Project-Based
WRITING

LIZ PRATHER

Foreword by Cris Tovani

Project-Based
WRITING

12/19

"planning
+ Doing"

Teaching Writers to
Manage Time and
Clarify Purpose

HEINEMANN
Portsmouth, NH

Heinemann

361 Hanover Street

Portsmouth, NH 03801–3912

www.heinemann.com

Offices and agents throughout the world

Excerpts from the Common Core State Standards © Copyright 2010. National Governors Association Center for Best Practices and Council of Chief State School Officers. All rights reserved.

Author photo by Paul Prather.

Library of Congress Cataloging-in-Publication Data

Name: Prather, Liz, author.
Title: Project-based writing : teaching writers to manage time and clarify
        purpose / Liz Prather.
Description: Portsmouth, NH : Heinemann, [2017]
Identifiers: LCCN 2017016653 | ISBN 9780325089805
Subjects: LCSH: English language—Composition and exercises—Study and
        teaching (Secondary)—United States. | English language—Composition and
        exercises—Study and teaching (Middle school)—United States. | Project
        method in teaching.
Classification: LCC LB1631 .P675 2017 | DDC 808/.0420712—dc23

LC record available at https://lccn.loc.gov/2017016653

Acquisitions Editor: Katie Wood Ray
Production Editor: Sean Moreau
Cover Design: Suzanne Heiser
Interior Design: Nicole Pollack
Typesetter: Shawn Girsberger
Manufacturing: Steve Bernier

Printed in the United States of America on acid-free paper
21 20 19 18 17 PAH 1 2 3 4 5

This book is dedicated to the memory of my grandmother,
Blanche Mary Roberts Smoot, who taught at The White Chapel School,
a one-room school on Twin Creek Road in Owen County, Kentucky.
A generous and graceful woman, she loved art, music, poetry,
and children.

CNTENTS

read/ annotate [handwritten annotation]

FREWORD

Thankfully, I selfishly agreed to write the foreword for this book. Not only did it mean I could read it before anyone else, but I could also see how another teacher implements writing instruction using a project-based format. By page seven, I was annotating comments like, "I love the voice." "She is so honest." "I can try this idea tomorrow." Jealously, I wanted to be the author of the book, not just the foreword!

By Chapter 3, the jealousy was gone and I was captivated. I thought to myself, *This teacher-author knows me. She knows my struggles. She knows what I care about as a writing teacher, and most importantly, she knows the wide range of students I teach.* Author Liz Prather shows readers how to balance authentic, engaging writing instruction with the responsibility of meeting standards to prepare students for college and beyond. She understands that choice drives engagement and that when students have a purpose or an opportunity to investigate something they are curious about, the desire to write well increases.

There are many reasons to read this book, but I'd like to highlight two—one for teachers and one for their students:

> **Reason #1:** *As a teacher, I will take risks to try new ideas if there are manageable ways for me to accomplish the new learning.*

I'm guessing that one reason teachers don't immediately glom onto project-based instruction is the fear of its complexity. For those who don't want to implement a pure project-based writing and learning model, Prather provides differentiated implementation options. Using her adaptations, readers can decide whether they want to dip their toe into the water or go for the full 500-meter swim.

Having taught striving readers and writers my whole career, this book provides support for teachers who have kids who won't write or think they can't write. *Project-Based Writing: Teaching Writers to Manage Time and Clarify Purpose* is so much more than a collection of ideas or units of study. Think authenticity—not a checklist of steps. Prather provides many examples that help teachers set up and manage the writing students will do. She demonstrates how teachers can harness the power of authentic audiences to induce risk taking and revision.

Prather has been in our shoes. She understands that writing is hard—and trying to teach someone else how to do it well is even harder. She empathizes with us because she, too, has handed back assignments that took the whole weekend to grade, only to have students focus on their point total as they promptly pitched their work into the trash. She's experienced the cruel reality that just because students turn in writing, it doesn't mean they actually care about the work they've done.

Like a lot of teachers, I'm always on the quest to consistently provide purposeful work and authentic audiences for whom students can write. I search to find better ways to help kids care about their writing enough to move beyond the *one and done* attitude. I struggle to balance the demands of a school setting with the work of real writers. And like all teachers, I want to help students write better, faster. This book is full of practical, manageable ideas that show teachers how to layer in systems and structures that will enhance planning routines and improve the quality of student writing.

> **Reason #2:** *Students will take ownership of their writing when they are afforded authentic reasons to write and shown the habits of real writers in the world.*

Prather honors the craft of teaching. She asks herself two questions that serve as a litmus test: Does this allow my students to direct their own learning? Am I showing students how writers work in the real world? Prather provides models for readers so they can shift the responsibility of writing well from the teacher to the student. She pulls away the curtain so readers can see how she develops students' reverence for their writing processes. Along the way, readers are learning how to develop the serious habits of writers.

As in life, in order for project-based writing to be successful, students have to learn how to project manage—a skill that all successful adults need. But there are many more soft skills that Prather weaves throughout the book—skills that aren't found on state or national assessments like persevering, being vulnerable, communicating clearly, pitching ideas, increasing endurance, and using failure as a means to learn. These are only some of the red threads woven throughout this book. Mastering these skills serves students as learners, but more importantly, they serve them way beyond high school graduation.

Prather's humor and practicality make *Project-Based Writing* a pragmatic and useful read. While glancing at the table of contents, I feared the ideas would be overwhelming. Instead, I found concrete ways to challenge my students. As I read, I found myself emotionally engaged—truly entertained. What I appreciated even more than being entertained was being cognitively engaged. Every time I picked up the book and read, I felt smarter.

We all know that writing is difficult. Defaulting to what real writers do, modeling authentic strategies, and providing opportunities for students to do real work will save us. That's the beauty of this book. You don't have to implement every idea to see growth in your students. There are all sizes of ideas here. Yes, I understand that reading professionally sometimes takes a back-seat to the day-to-day work that has to get done. Teachers are busy people! But take heart. Reading and thinking about how to use this book will be well worth your time. You will quite likely be the person students remember as the one who taught them how to write!

—Cris Tovani

ACKNOWLEDGMENTS

The story of my writing life is a complicated, meandering one, but the story of my teaching life begins and ends in just one place: the Morehead Writing Project (MWP) at Morehead State University. In 1994, I was a second-year high school English teacher who was accepted to a four-week Summer Institute for writing teachers. During that summer, I was introduced to Peter Elbow, Donald Murray, Barry Lane, Nancie Atwell, and a whole world of professional literature about writing and writing pedagogy. I will always be grateful for the encouragement and mentorship of then-director Dr. Wayne Willis, who invited me to participate that summer and who has both inspired and cheered me on for my entire career.

It was also at the MWP I met Dr. Nancy Peterson, who became the director after Wayne. She believed writing to be a transformative, powerful, political act, and she worked hard to bridge the gap between writing theory and practical classroom experience. She urged the hundreds of eastern Kentucky teachers whose lives she touched to theorize their practice and to nurture themselves as writers despite the daily struggles of teaching. She influenced my professional career more than any other person.

It was also through the MWP I met Barry Lane in 1996 and to whom I reached out two years ago with the idea for this book. He gave me advice and encouragement then and continues to be a kindred spirit and hero.

I would also like to thank my friend and current MWP director, Deanna Mascle, who has given me numerous opportunities to grow professionally. I am equally grateful to the current MWP Summer Institute codirectors Brandis Carlson, Vicki Moriarity, Jared Salyers, and Leslie Workman, and the teachers of the 2016 Summer Institute (Georgina Anderson, Sabrina Brandenburg, Dallas Cox, Beth Garrison, Sheina Kegley, and Seth Thatcher), who embraced project-based writing and carried out action research based on my professional work with their students.

I am grateful for the professionalism and camaraderie of all the educators with whom I've had the honor to work at Morehead State and the Montgomery and Fayette County school districts, but I am specifically thankful for the encouragement, love, support, and quite possibly the longest-running professional text conversation in modern history with my fellow teachers Austen Reilley, Amy Gilliam, Stephanie Smith, and Risha Mullins.

I could not have written this book without the support of Bryne Jacobs, my principal at Lafayette High School, and my dear colleague Louise Gash for selflessly absorbing some of my workload when I needed it the most.

I am indebted to my student Sarah Hall, who gave me honest and thoughtful written evaluations of each step of this process while she was my student and afterward as an undergraduate at Transylvania University. I would also like to thank the long-suffering but totally game writing class on whom I first tried full-scale project-based writing. To Serena, Sarah, Margaux, Aidan, Victoria, Christopher, Taylor, Rayny, Kynnadie, and Hannah—you are the most.

At the ideation and incubation stage of this book, I was fortunate to have the encouragement of friends and fellow teachers Vickie Moriarity, Chris McCurry, and Sasha Reinhardt, who also read an early draft and gave me apt critical feedback.

To my best reader, sounding board, and editor, Katie Ray, I am so grateful for you believing in this book and showing me the straight path through it. No one has ever read my work so closely and clearly.

And finally, I will always be grateful and indebted to my husband Paul, a great writer, a brave thinker, and the best storyteller in twenty counties. Thank you for your editing, but mostly, your patience and love.

1

The Journey to Project–Based Writing

At no time in Kentucky's history had more attention been paid to the art of writing than in 1990, my first year of teaching. The previous year, the Council for Better Education, along with several boards of education, five school districts, and twenty-two students, sued the governor, the speaker of the house, and the State Board of Education, stating Kentucky's educational system was financially a mess and educationally even worse (*Rose v. Council for Better Education* 1989).

The Kentucky Supreme Court declared Kentucky schools unconstitutional, and the resulting legislation, the Kentucky Education Reform Act (KERA), remains one of the most comprehensive education reforms in United States history (Miller 1990).

One of the many changes legislated by KERA was the implementation of a statewide writing portfolio, the scores of which counted as 14 percent of each school's accountability index (Whitford and Jones 2000). As a result, teachers scrambled for materials and lesson plans to meet the demands of this new assessment. Writing process choo choo trains chugged across the bulletin boards of Kentucky elementary schools, and graphic organizers for webbing, bubbling, and mapping were churned out by the hundreds.

The writing process—as individual as each student—quickly became systemized. Teachers soon found themselves teaching the portfolio instead of teaching student writers.

Because the writing requirement was cross-curricular, students collected writing samples from every class. During their fourth-, eighth- and twelfth-grade years, they selected their best samples to be placed in a folder and scored holistically by their teachers using a statewide rubric (Spalding and Cummins 1998).

To score the portfolios, English teachers trained their whole school staff, from counselors to administrators to the football coach, on how to use the state rubric. This codification further cemented the notion that the writing process had, in fact, become a product itself. What started as a laudable endeavor—to cultivate writing across the curriculum—ended up as an entrenched writing recipe imposed on thousands of children as "The Writing Process." Predictably, the portfolios were short on creativity and long on compliance.

Jump forward a few years. I was visiting my niece, who had recently graduated high school. We were looking at pictures of her various graduation events. One picture was of a bonfire in the middle of a field with kids dancing around it. In their hands were manila folders.

"What are you burning?" I asked her.

"Our senior writing portfolios," she said.

WRITING AS AN INDIVIDUAL PROCESS

Today I was sitting in traffic on my way home from work, listening to the news. I heard a sound bite of New Jersey Governor Chris Christie saying that national teachers' unions deserved a punch in the face because they were apparently so difficult to work with (CNN Politics 2015). The night before I had had a discussion with my husband about how our own Kentucky teachers' union was struggling to work with state government to find solutions to fully fund our pension system.

When I heard the sound bite, I pulled out my smart phone (I was at a traffic light!) and did a little Safari research. I quickly found an article on the *New York Times* website about Christie's track record with New Jersey educators (Applebome 2010). More information.

A topic of personal interest, a conversation with my husband, a sound bite, a long traffic light, some Internet research, and I was writing in my head. As I drove home, I free-associated. By the time I arrived, I had what my students and I would call a "zero draft," a disorganized mishmash of ideas. I went to my home office, opened my laptop, and typed up a few notes. Maybe it will be a blog post, maybe a letter to the editor about funding teachers' pensions, maybe a letter to my legislator, but, as I wrote, I was discovering what I wanted to say and what I thought.

That is my process.

When a writing idea presents itself to me out of thin air, a gift (or burden) from the universe, there's a cognitive spark accompanied by an urge to get black on white as fast as I can. An idea has presented itself in the form of a hunch, an exigent moment. My swirling thoughts are unformed and erratic, but colored with anticipation.

Writers write in a state of what Romantic poet John Keats called "negative capability," the capacity to exist in ambiguity without reaching for the comfort of known facts and forms for the purpose of creation (Rollins 1958, 193). Creation demands the ability to sit with the mysterious and abide in the unknown. To create anything, the poet must trust that even though she's never gone down this particular road before, she will find her way. This ability is the beginning of original thought.

These steps follow what neuroscientists know about the cognitive stages of creativity: preparation, incubation, illumination, and verification. Rarely do these stages occur in a linear course; often recursive, multiple aha moments are embedded in a cloud of mental wandering, ultimately leading to an intentionally crafted product.

In other words, writing begins as a hot mess of ideas in the head of a writer who is casting about for the right words, fumbling for images and logical sequences to string it all together. Wrong steps, blind alleys, dead-ends. This is what we know about the writing process: it's highly individualized and messy, couched in equal parts success and failure.

CUTE, SINGLE WRITING PROCESS SEEKS ROBUST PROJECT MANAGEMENT FRAMEWORK

For years, the teacher in me was unable to articulate in a lesson plan what I did intuitively as a writer. How could I create a system to teach such a messy, highly personal skill without damaging the skill or discouraging the person? Perhaps I couldn't delineate the process from the product or perhaps I had conflated the phases of my process into a single rush of creative impulse. Whatever my rationalization, I ended up teaching writing in a fairly artificial way, far removed from the reality of how my own ideas and language worked together to form text.

Thus, I taught writing like a teacher, not like a writer.

I started with "The Writing Law"—forms, formulas, graphic organizers, and requirements—the very thing Keats would have cited as a barrier to creative thought. I told students they needed three of this and one of that. I taught three points and five paragraphs. I taught grammar and vocabulary as isolated activities. I taught through keyholes and hourglasses and hamburgers. Mad Libs for essays. I gave them models and mentor texts to show them how it should be done, and I drew up gloriously detailed and rigorously aligned rubrics to score their work.

I gave them my ideas, my assignments, my models, my texts, my rubrics. And then I was baffled when I got dry, surface essays riddled with mechanical errors.

I could blame the system. After all, my principal wanted two grades a week recorded into the district's electronic grade book, but learning, especially in the case of writing, is occasionally just sitting in a chair staring out the window. How would I grade that? How could I write a lesson plan for cognitive anarchy, rule breaking, and risk—the foreplay of all serious writing products?

In a passage in Ernest Hemingway's *A Moveable Feast*, he discusses his own creative incubation habits:

> But sometimes when I was starting a new story and I could not get it going, I would sit in front of the fire and squeeze the peel of the little oranges into the edge of the flame and watch the sputter of blue that they made. I would stand and look out over the roofs of Paris and think, "Do not worry. You have always written before and you will write now." (1964, 8)

Where were my oranges? My nice fire? The roofs of Paris? And what does proficiency in peel squeezing look like?

I needed a framework for learning and writing that would keep my students accountable and engaged, but would allow them to read and write from their own passions and support the recursive switchbacks and failure I experienced in my own writing process. I needed a system that could manage the project of writing while protecting the process of discovery. A system that would allow my students to maintain a writing practice while helping them with deadlines, word counts, submission guidelines—all the things that real writers contend with on a regular basis.

How could I build an instructional support that would allow for the failure necessary for growing writers, but also instill in them a knowledge of time management, goal setting, and production?

ENTER PROJECT-BASED LEARNING

Around this time, I was introduced, by some flash of serendipity, to the concept of project-based learning, the idea of learning by doing. I was invited, along with several teachers from my school, to visit nearby Danville Independent High

School, one of the first schools in Kentucky to attempt a large-scale project-based learning program.

In the last decade, project-based learning has become a laudable model for student choice and learner-directed education. The framework is simple: students choose a problem to solve or a question to answer, and through self-directed investigation, they solve the problem or answer the question and learn new skills along the way. Students work in groups and individually. At the end of the project, students unveil a product that represents what they've learned. And they show off that project to people outside the classroom—parents, scientists, city planners, engineers, or businesspeople (Krajcik and Blumenfeld 2006).

PBL

The projects are complex, multitiered, nonlinear, and always real-world. Students are involved in every level of the project, from the framing of the initial problem, to setting goals, to determining instructional activities. Teachers facilitate these projects, but they don't control the process or even issue any explicit goals. The students do all that good, good work.

do we do this at CHS?

The research on project-based learning concludes that students in this instructional framework feel more ownership of their own learning and report having higher attendance, more self-reliance, and more retention of core subject material. In addition, students gain greater problem-solving abilities when learning information through its application (Vega 2015; Thomas 2000; Krajcik and Blumenfeld 2006).

Imagine that.

The Danville teachers started with an English–science hybrid class where students built their own desks, designed catapults, wrote comic books, and learned city planning design using basic geometry. It was a practical approach that focused on application of skills, not just memorization of facts. Students also learned organizational and management skills beyond the basic curriculum that could be applied to all problem-solving. All learning in their classrooms stemmed from, and in relation to, a student-selected question or problem.

In a true project-based classroom, students are in control. If this gives you hives, I understand, but it's not the frat-party-meets-prison-break you might imagine. *Student-centered* means that students' questions become the focus of learning. Their desire to learn creates a need to know, and in the midst of that energy, they solve problems, analyze data, think critically, and develop soft skills like self-control and tenacity.

how do we do this in Humanities 12?

Although the teacher may directly teach students how to analyze data, draw conclusions, and present their findings, he doesn't tell them *what* data to analyze, *what* conclusions to draw, or *what* findings they might discover. For those of us who paid attention in theory classes, this is classic constructivist pedagogy: students form new knowledge in the process of investigation based on what they already know and believe.

In project-based learning, students cannot embark on a project that relies on information they already know with outcomes they have already encountered. That's why the brave new world of project-based learning is so fresh and appealing. And why it is so terrifying.

True project-based learning is based in the unknown and requires students to work to find their footing along with answers to their questions. Because students determine the direction of their own learning, the project-based classroom does not rely on prepackaged worksheets, scripted lessons, or teacher-led activities. The learning is unpredictable and requires more student self-sufficiency and responsibility than a traditional classroom, as well as more flexibility and versatility from the teacher, who moves from being the central figure in the front of the class to being more of a coach on the sidelines.

Teachers monitor the framework of learning, including students' timelines, goal sheets, contracts, and individual evaluations. Teachers also provide individual, small-group, or whole-group instruction by necessity or on demand. The assessment is all formative, as the students learn to manage each project with a growing body of skills. Students evaluate and reflect on their growth throughout the project. In most project-based learning, a student-developed rubric is used to assess the summative product.

Studies over the last three decades (Thomas 2000; Vega 2015) support the value of project-based learning for student growth and achievement, but for me, the most appealing part of this instructional model is that the classroom feels less like school and more like a laboratory or a studio or a think tank. The real-word trappings of project-based learning reinforce the authenticity of this approach. The projects are more robust and engaging than any simulated problems students have seen in textbooks. The students respond to this sparkle with true engagement. This is something new. Is this real school?

It's the kind of platform that causes this scenario to happen daily: a kid, deep in thought, activity, study, research, looks up as the bell rings, disbelieving his time is gone. This class always goes so fast, he might mumble as he puts away his notebook, his laptop, his tools.

The teacher smiles. That's pure gold.

ENTER PROJECT-BASED WRITING

Project-based learning was the framework I'd been looking for to simultaneously protect the creative processes of 148 students while helping them learn to manage long-term writing projects, the kind of projects they would be doing in college or in a career. I realized by transferring the project-based learning tenets into a regular English classroom, my students could develop skills to become independent readers and writers.

Every kind of writing is its own unique problem. Writing is the quintessential project, in fact, of organization, language, purpose, and thought. In addition, a project-based instructional framework allows students to write using their own processes but manage time and tasks within the schema and structure of a project management model. Student writers need practice in managing a project, like writing an argument or short story, from beginning to end while retaining their autonomy and creativity. This kind of external system could serve as kind of a compass for the journey.

In project-based writing, students manage their writing project with systemized external supports like pitches, proposals, project goals, and schedules, but the process remains wholly the student's, and the resulting product is also the student's from conception to rendering to delivery. The steps of all writing projects are clearly parallel with the steps of project-based learning.

WRITING	PROJECT-BASED LEARNING
Idea incubation	Inquiry
Framing an idea for a piece of writing	Framing a question for a project
Research, drafting, feedback	Research, investigation, testing
Writing a final draft	Completing a finished project
Publication	Presentation

From an English teacher's perspective, the marriage of writing and project-based learning was a dreamworld of student choice and purposeful problem-solving. Of course, students need to know the parameters of good writing. They also need to know how forms, modes, and mentor texts function and why an analysis of these existing models is a defensible activity, but these exercises are secondary to writers' ideas, their thoughts, their theories, and their lives. And all the elements of literacy that may have once been taught in isolation—reading, analysis, grammar, expository design, documentation, research, tone, diction, syntax—could be taught in the service of a student-selected project with a generous sidecar of real motivation and a built-in audience.

Using minilessons to teach skills like documentation or summary in the larger framework of project-based writing gives those lessons relevance and context. Much of my teaching lacked relevancy other than, "You'll need to know this for college." That kind of thinking is similar to giving a toddler a driver's manual and telling her that someday those rules will be very, very important.

To a student who has been awakened politically and now wants to write a political blog, teaching a minilesson about how to craft a counterclaim is like giving her the keys to the kingdom. She has a need that has generated a desire to learn. It's at that intersection she will meet you, eager and engaged, to learn about how to make a sound argument. Every kid, no matter who she is, where she lives, how checked out she is, or what her skill level might be, has a similar intersection.

Teaching writing through a project-based approach did require flexibility, ongoing reflection, and a giant shift in my instructional paradigm. But along the way, I discovered I was not teaching writing as much as I was teaching writers to persevere in the face of dead-ends and wrong turns. The lessons reached far beyond my classroom, engendering confidence in my students and paying huge dividends of autonomy and independence.

THIS SOUNDS A WHOLE LOT LIKE WRITING WORKSHOP BECAUSE IT IS

At this point, you might be saying, hmm, how is this any different from reading-writing workshop?

Indeed, the research of Peter Elbow, Nanci Atwell, and Lucy Calkins shaped my formative pedagogy. Writing workshop and project-based writing are both focused on the fundamental goal of letting students write about their lives in genuine contexts for real-world audiences. The two instructional models are similar as well: both are student centered, both use conferences with peers and teachers, both use small- and whole-group activities, and both mimic an artistic community.

Both of these approaches are also holistic. They both support teaching skills and content in the larger context of student choice. Writing workshop is centered in the writing process, whereas project-based writing, although nurturing the individual process, is framed by the project itself. In *The Art of Teaching Writing*, Calkins (1994) defines writing workshop as "an ongoing, predictable studio in which youngsters could develop and pursue their own important purposes as a writer" (96). Similarly, in project-based writing, all instruction is dependent on the individual project, and the responsibility shifts from teacher to student.

Project-based writing doesn't just teach a student how to understand her individual writing process, but how to manage the large, sometimes unwieldy, project of writing as well. In project-based writing, the best elements of reading-writing workshop are augmented by the intentional framework of project management.

I like to think it is the best of both worlds.

As a writer, I have deadlines. From my editors, I'm given a word count to which I must adhere. When I prepare a manuscript for submission to a literary journal, there are submission guidelines and formatting requirements. In college, professors assign writing assignments at the beginning of the semester, and students are required to research, document, and write largely on their own.

Without a system of management for tackling such a project, many students often wait until the last minute because the prospect of starting and finishing a large project is so daunting. Although reading-writing workshop certainly lays the groundwork for independence, project-based writing provides students with transferable tools such as how to pitch a creative idea, how to write a proposal, how to schedule and manage time for a large project, how to give and receive feedback on creative projects, and how to evaluate one's own work to revise for publication.

HOW TO USE THIS BOOK

This book represents my experiences and thoughts about project-based writing, as well as practical tips about how to implement a project-based writing framework in your own English classroom.

For purposes of full disclosure, I did not attempt to execute a full-fledged, project-based writing design all at once. At the start of my teaching career, I spent five years teaching writing in a fairly traditional way, that is to say, I taught writing form first. After I participated in a National Writing Project Summer Institute and was introduced to Atwell's reading-writing workshop, I incorporated those strategies into my classroom. After I was introduced to project-based learning in 2010, I added one or two project-based elements to the main core of my classroom structure, but I was teaching at a school where classes met every day for fifty minutes, and it was a challenge to find the uninterrupted studio time students needed to write.

It wasn't until I began teaching at a large urban high school where I took a position in an embedded arts program with a writing-only class that I finally stepped away from form-first instruction altogether. I had smaller classes and ninety-minute blocks. For the first time in my teaching career, I was able to teach writing as a writer.

Since then I have modified its scope every year to meet the needs of my individual classes, even though the seven-step process remains the same. When I taught a writing class with forty students, for example, I had to modify whole-group activities, like pitching and inquiry, into smaller-group exercises, but the project-based writing model worked because students were engaged in their own self-selected projects.

It's not necessary to supplant your current curriculum or replace your instructional model to give students a small taste of the project-based world. Adopting just a few of these strategies will easily increase engagement and support differentiation for writers. My students complete six writing project cycles in an academic year, but students can benefit from learning the project management system with just one.

Project-based writing is not an all-or-nothing model. Many isolated elements of this system can be adopted and implemented singularly to provide students with autonomy and choice without embracing the whole framework. For example, here are some alternatives to whole-hog project-based writing that you can mull over while we go through the steps in this book:

- **One day a week:** Carve out one day per week when students can pursue a writing project of their own choice. Teach students the framework and use the project as an anchor activity throughout a semester or academic year.

- **Two-week cycle:** Using the techniques for compressing time you'll find in this book, dedicate two weeks to a single writing cycle to introduce the project management tools to students.

- **One six- or nine-week unit:** If your school's curriculum is built around six-week or nine-week instructional periods, the framework of project-based writing can fit neatly into a unit. Once students learn the steps of project-based writing in a defined, intentionally led unit, they can apply elements of it, such as pitching or project scheduling, to any long writing assignment they will encounter.

- **20Time:** Google asks its employees to spend 20 percent of their time at work to concentrate on a pet project. Sasha Reinhardt, a middle school English language arts teacher friend of mine, recently borrowed from corporate Google's time management model and the research of Daniel Pink to introduce 20Time in her classroom for writing instruction through a project-based learning approach (Pink 2011). Each week for her twelve-week grading period, 20 percent of class time is devoted to project-based writing and 80 percent of the time is spent on a traditional unit of study.

Each teacher must come to the project-based universe on her own terms, using what this model has to offer within the structure of her classroom and (this is the most important part) her intimate knowledge of her students—where they are, how they learn, what they need. Knowing what works best for your students is the key to adopting any instructional framework.

Two questions guide all my teaching:

1. Does this allow my students to direct their own learning?

2. Is this how writers work in the real world?

But there are countless other considerations: What about the student who wants his learning spooned into his open mouth, who has no desire to write anything, or honestly, even pick up a pencil? And how do you have a facilitating conference with individual students when you have forty kids in each class? What are the logistics for establishing effective say-back groups? How do you grade students when everyone is working at her own pace on her own project? How do you make sure you are covering all the standards? How do you answer the administrator who claims you've given up teaching and are allowing students to teach themselves? (Yes!) How do you explain the efficacy of this system to parents?

I have asked myself all those questions, and although I may not know your unique situation, I do have some practical advice on executing a project-based writing model in your classroom in whatever form you elect to implement it. This book is designed to allow you to adopt either all or some of the elements of project-based writing. Perhaps your classroom already runs smoothly with reading-writing workshop, and you want to introduce a few project management strategies. Perhaps you want students to choose their topics, but you aren't ready for them to develop their own evaluation tools. Perhaps you love the idea of the proposal, but you have a group of students who aren't mature enough to handle the individual studio time.

For these reasons, Chapters 3 to 10 explain all the steps in the project-based writing process, but I have also scattered a number of "switch points" throughout the chapters. On a railroad line, a train can be diverted to another track through the use of a switch point. I like this simple metaphor for mini-implementation because each teacher can choose to make a small detour into the project management world without leaving the train they're on.

A NEW PARADIGM

Whatever form project-based writing takes in your classroom, you will have moments where everything you've held dear as an educator will be challenged. When I began project-based writing, I had to reconfigure my teaching style to truly understand and help my student writers. The framework also required me to deliver writing instruction on the spot, often during conferences, to provide students with lessons on the skills as they were needed. I had to retool my whole approach to classroom management, classroom arrangement, and grades. As a person who has difficulty stepping away from a lesson plan, I had to rethink how I delivered instruction. There were more "stop, drop, and teach" moments because student learning is built on the "I need to know this now" wellsprings instead of the "You'll need to know this someday" threat.

The term *kaizen*, a Japanese business philosophy, most closely describes the approach my teaching now takes. Although *kaizen* loosely means "continuous improvement" or "change for the better," the term also encompasses the concepts of efficiency, waste reduction, and just-in-time delivery of materials for the purposes of increased satisfaction in the workplace and success in the marketplace. The traditional tenets of Japanese *kaizen* are personal discipline and a culture of teamwork, but the larger goal of the philosophy is to exact small changes to contribute to the overall success of the business (Maurer 2014).

In the past, I would lay out large, cumbersome units that taught isolated concepts. There was a lot of cognitive, social, and educational waste in this approach. But within the *kaizen* principles, the skills and concepts are taught as they are needed, which provides students with an immediate cognitive latch on which to buckle their newly discovered skill.

Every project, every student, every day is different, invigorating, challenging. For the first three years, the approach demanded ongoing and honest reflection about my own practice of writing and teaching as well as continually requesting that my students give me feedback and make suggestions to "change for the better." Guiding students to their own discovery is difficult, but much more rewarding for both the teacher and his students.

I want my students to value clear expression, to develop a reverence for their own process, and to develop seriousness about the practice of writing, but also, along the way, to adopt a management framework they will use, in some rendering, for the rest of their lives. And in that way, project-based writing touches the very heart of what is best about the educational experience—curiosity, inquiry, motivation, and hard work. It also touches the very best of teaching—an authentic, individualized, student-centered practice.

Project-based writing then becomes the juncture of apprenticeship and self-discovery for both the student and the teacher. Both are on the road toward mastery of a skill, both writing and teaching, that perhaps neither will fully realize in a lifetime.

Oh, but the journey.

An Overview for Project-Based Writing:
A Framework in Seven Steps

When I first attempted project-based learning in the writing classroom, I recognized this framework could buoy the risky and recursive business of writing without damaging the writing processes of my students. But because the framework bears a great resemblance to almost all project management systems, I knew these skills could be used by my students throughout their college or career paths. Every element of this design is a highly transferrable schema that my students, as developing writers and thinkers, needed because it reflected the practices of mature writers and thinkers. The seven steps of the project-based writing framework I use in my classroom are:

- discovering an idea
- framing the work
- planning the work
- doing the work
- reframing the work
- finalizing the work
- revealing the work.

Before I crack open all the teacher moves to get project-based writing started in your classroom, I think it's important for you to see the process in action. Understanding any teaching framework only matters if you can picture the system doing powerful work in your students' lives and work. As an example of the project-based writing framework, let's take a look at Victoria, a typical seventeen-year-old senior in my class, and follow the seven steps of her project from declaring her own curiosities to the not-what-she-imagined final product.

DISCOVERING AN IDEA

The first step requires the student writer to discover a writing idea. I provide students dozens of generative writing assignments, but Victoria's project came squarely out of her experience as a teen—juggling friends, a full schedule of classes, an after-school fast-food job, and nascent romantic enterprises. Victoria, and her friend Aidan, who was also in my class, were passionate fans of hip-hop music. One day, they discovered their respective significant others didn't know much about hip-hop. Hip-hop was a subject that could hold their interest, a subject they already knew a little about, and a writing project for which they had a ready-made audience.

Victoria and Aidan started to sketch out a table of contents with numerous discussions about who would write what parts. The table of contents became an enormous, ever-expanding bulleted list that ballooned to nearly twelve chapters before Aidan decided he wanted to embark on his own project. This kind of negotiation and clarification happens a lot in the project-based classroom. It's an echo of the real-world nature of writing. So Victoria decided to pursue the project on her own.

FRAMING THE WORK

Framing the work requires students to pitch the idea to the class and also write a 300- to 500-word proposal to the teacher. To the class, Victoria pitched her idea (a two- to five-minute verbal pitch with five minutes afterward for the class to ask questions) as sort of an "Idiot's Guide to Hip-Hop" as well as a way for her to geek out over her favorite rappers and analyze the importance of hip-hop culture.

After the class voted and approved her project, she formalized her idea with a proposal, a short informational text that explained the genesis of her idea as well as what she wanted her final product to look and sound like, plus a few possible publication venues she would like to pursue when the project was finished.

She proposed a series of loosely connected "chapters" that she would publish on her personal blog. She wrote:

> Chapter 1 will be a genesis of hip-hop in late '70s with introduction to
> pop culture with Rappers Delight, a chapter on Eric B & Rakim to Nas, a
> chapter on Jay Z/Eminem/Lil Wayne: Rap Is Pop, and a chapter on Kanye

West, Rap as Capital-A Art. Keep in mind that these are extremely bare
outlines and the extensive amount of knowledge will make the chapters
much more in depth and exploratory than they appear right now. I'm
really passionate about this subject.

In her proposal, she conceded the project might be larger than she could handle. She was also worried she wouldn't have the credibility to write it. She wrote, "I'm concerned about my authority as a writer on this. I'll be doing LARGE amounts of research and hopefully I'll be able to fit everything into the chapters without (a) missing anything important or (b) sounding like a nerdy white kid who likes Run–DMC."

PLANNING THE WORK

The next step is planning the work, which includes setting goals and scheduling tasks for the project. Victoria easily broke the larger project into small, manageable tasks and delineated time for research, outlining, drafting, and revising. She blocked out her studio time in class into equal parts research and writing, but she wasn't as clear on how to set goals for the finished product. Setting goals at this stage of the game is asking students to envision what qualities the finished product will possess. Goal statements are important because their passion for this project will be at its height at this point in the project cycle, but their vision for what they want the end result to be may or may not be clear.

"What qualities do you want the finished draft of this piece to have?" I said to Victoria as we conferenced and worked together to come up with her four product goals.

"I want it to be fantastic?" she said.

"That's pretty broad, right? You know a lot about this topic, but you're going to do some research too. Could quality research be a goal for the project?"

"It could, but I figure that a lot of the stuff I read about, I might not use," she said.

"That's still research. Anything you read is considered research, and all of that goes into your project library, even things you don't use."

"Research as a goal just sounds too big. How will people know if I've researched anything?"

"By your knowledge of the subject, for starts," I said.

"OK, how about informational content? Yeah, that sounds good," she said and wrote down *content* on the top of her goal sheet.

"I'm also hearing in your proposal that you're worried about your tone. You want it to be authentic?" I said.

"I want it to be cool and conversational too. Not like a Wikipedia article," she said.

"That's definitely a goal then," I advised. "Write that down."

"I need more coffee," she said.

After some deliberation, she came up with informational content, conversational tone, clear organization, and appropriate mechanics for her four goals.

DOING THE WORK

The next step of the project-based flow is actually doing the work of writing. On Victoria's timeline, she set a goal to finish three "chapters" for the inquiry draft workshop. Although I recognized her passion for the topic, I could tell she was struggling to articulate in the proposal what her focus or main idea was for the piece. I advised her to spend some time developing a central claim through freewriting, but she decided she would start writing the piece and hoped the purpose would present itself along the way.

As a writer, I know that writing without knowing the central claim or writing toward an unspecified point that hasn't revealed itself yet is an authentic station of the writing process.

Victoria embarked on the project with gusto and amassed a great deal of research on hip-hop, but she was never able to find her groove (forgive me). During our weekly conferences, I could tell she was having trouble discovering the thematic core on which to hang all her research. I read over what she had, a tangle of music history and disconnected facts, a good zero draft that needed a central focus.

"Is there something here that is more important to focus on or do you still just want it to be an informational hip-hop guide?" I asked her during a conference.

"I just want to finish it," she said.

I wanted her to consider these questions before she submitted the piece to the class for inquiry, but ultimately, Victoria was in charge of her project. What puzzled me the most about her drafts were the breaks in tone, from formal to informal. The organization was also hard to follow with facts all jammed together, connected only with some snide comments about hipsters or rhetorical questions meant to amuse or break the fourth wall.

We had several conferences where we discussed tone and organization, two of the elements she seemed to be battling. Her original tone was flip and sharp, featuring her sassy wit and pop culture references she used with ease and accuracy, but I also noticed another voice emerging—one that was more solemn, candid, and somewhat nostalgic.

She wrote, "I was born in a small eastern Kentucky town, and moved to the big city of Lexington when I was six after my parents' divorce. That part is simple and easy enough said."

Her syntax initially was more complex, but I noticed she was delving into shorter, more declarative sentences, using diction that was simple, straightforward, personal. I pointed out these shifts, circling several examples of diction and syntax that moved the tone.

"Does this shift need to be explored or revised or what?"

"I don't know. Leave me alone, Mom," she joked as she sat in the dark corner of our classroom library in an old Army coat, her dark hair cropped close to her head, listening to music as she wrote.

"Are you trying to cover too much ground in a short piece?"

"I have to turn something in," she said finally. "And I've already spent two weeks researching and writing this thing."

Let me add that these moments of direct instruction and writerly mentorship are critical in project-based writing. In addition to whole-class or small-group mini-lessons that I execute throughout the project cycle when I see instructional needs arise, these microlessons—targeted, impromptu, intentionally delivered through questions, often in a crouched position—represent the largest part of my project-based writing curriculum. There are no plans for microlessons, only the spontaneous gut responses of one writer-teacher person to one writer-student person.

After using project-based writing for five years, I still feel the urge to fix things for my students, and I do daily redirect students who, I feel, are biting off

Is the teacher reading the whole thing?

Project-Based Writing

more project than they can successfully chew. However, the lessons they learn from flailing around in their own process will be far more lasting.

[margin note: let them work through it on their own. Balance between structure + enabling failure?]

To me, it seemed obvious that the piece she wanted to write, perhaps needed to write, was much smaller, more personal. What had this music really meant to her, an Appalachian kid growing up in the mountains of eastern Kentucky, listening to her uncle's wailing renditions of Creedence Clearwater Revival or to WSIP, Paintsville, Kentucky's country music station?

She wrote, "At odds with myself and my entire life, I gave up on music because there was nothing I could get behind. I was searching for music that I understood, that spoke to me, and in finding none, I lost contact with the form of media in its entirety for several years."

That was a voice that sounded authentic, one I hoped she would pursue in her rewrite.

REFRAMING THE WORK

[margin note: what is this?]

The next step in the project-based writing flow is submitting an inquiry draft to the class along with inquiry questions, then getting feedback from the class, and reframing the work based on the data received from their annotations and verbal responses.

When Victoria turned in the first chapter to the class, she asked questions about the focus of the writing. Remember, her four original goals were content, tone, organization, and mechanics, but she knew the focus was fuzzy, so she asked, "How would you describe the purpose of these pieces?" and "Is there a single focus that runs through them? If so, what is it?"

She couldn't really determine where and how the pieces lost purpose, but she knew that they did. During the say-back session, the class, predictably, told her the pieces lacked unity and pointed out specific places in her text where they felt lost, where they felt she jumped from one topic to the next without taking the reader with her.

[margin note: — structure?]

The class praised her efforts, however, for tone and pointed out the areas they felt were the strongest in her piece. The worst parts, they reported, were when she appropriated a music historian's persona, a voice that sounded forced and unnatural. They liked her own voice speaking directly to the reader about hip-

[margin note: How is the class primed to give feedback?]

hop's influence on her life, specifically those moments I had pointed out earlier, that were nostalgic and personal.

Later in her reflection, Victoria recognized they were right. "My first misstep was that the planning I thought I had wasn't really planning at all. I had no idea what it was going to be about. So I basically wrote a Wikipedia article about the origins of rap and then realized about a week before workshop that there was nothing artistic about it, it was just a collective bunch of facts."

She was crestfallen after the feedback she received from the class, but she quickly recalibrated. We had about two weeks left in the project cycle, and she wanted to use the research she had amassed to write something smaller, tighter, and more centrally focused.

This part of project-based writing is fascinating because it most closely mimics the work of real writers—the adjustments and fine-tuning, the midstream arbitration with one's own vision, the heartbreak when you realize that X is just not working and that you've spent two weeks writing material you ultimately can't use. Carol Bly in *Beyond the Writers' Workshop* says that, besides writers, research scientists are the only other people who understand that they are doing all this work but it might come to naught (2001, xvii). With project-based writing, this learning about failure, balance, navigation, and loss of forward momentum is the lesson.

After a couple of days sitting in the corner of the room with a scowl on her face, growling at any one who attempted to comfort her, Victoria realized the piece she wanted to write, or maybe needed to write, was much smaller than her original idea.

Instead of attempting to encompass all of hip-hop, Victoria chose a single album through which she could deconstruct her development as a teen and lover of hip-hop. She selected Lauryn Hill's seminal album, *The Miseducation of Lauryn Hill*, as the focal point of a powerful piece that was part personal essay and part critical analysis of Hill's musical blending of R&B, hip-hop, and soul. Her original title, "So You Want to Have an Opinion on Hip-Hop: A Crash Course in Hip-Hop for Your Modern Day Hipster," changed to "A 17-Year-Old Kentuckian and Lauryn Hill: The Lessons I Learned Through Miseducation" signaled that the scope had been narrowed, the focus shifted from public service to personal exploration, and the voice had finally settled on home.

FINALIZING THE WORK

In the penultimate step on the project-based flow, students write a reflection about their project and create an individual evaluation tool that their peers use to score their final product.

In her personal reflection, Victoria wrote, "I am beyond happy with the piece that I wrote. I feel like I finally grasped what I was trying to say about hip-hop, I loved writing an homage to Lauryn Hill, and I feel like I really put myself into the piece. I need to learn a lot about direction and my authority as a writer. I'm proud of what I produced but extremely disappointed at all the time I wasted writing things that I didn't even use."

The turning point of Victoria's writing process was grounded in her discovery that Lauryn Hill's miseducation was parallel and a part of her own childhood, fraught with abandonment and addiction. At six years old, Victoria had moved from a little town in the Appalachian Mountains to Lexington, Kentucky, an urban hive by her lights. Her geographical displacement, along with her parents' divorce, created a sense of longing and loss in Victoria that she recognized on Hill's album.

Along with writing a reflection of the final product, Victoria also developed an individual evaluation tool that allowed her classmates to score her on mechanics, organization, tone, and the analysis of the music as it related to her life.

REVEALING THE WORK

Victoria submitted this new 3,510-word essay to the class in a process we call "community score," where each student evaluates every other student's final product based on the individual evaluation categories that writer has chosen. In addition to scoring each final product, each student also provides a short argument using textual evidence to justify their score. This short argument provides further data to help students revise the pieces before the final step of revealing the work to the world.

Victoria's essay had been completely overhauled when she submitted it to community score, and the class loved it. One student wrote about the final piece, "There are still issues with the grammar, the title could be stronger, and you use rhetorical questions (there are seven in the first eight paragraphs) more than you should, but combining the album with your own life story works like no other piece you've written this year. There are moments of such perfect clarity (the last sentence) that I wish every piece you wrote was on this level. It has come a long way from the wiki-comedy we read at workshop. It feels real, and it feels like this is what you've had inside you all year. It's great."

Throughout her essay, Victoria compares and contrasts Hill's tracks to the complex relationship Victoria has with her mother, and ultimately, the relationship she has with her own developing self.

Here's a small sample from the section where she analyzes Hill's song, "Doo Wop (That Thing)":

> Is there anything even left to be said about this track? In one of the baddest female empowerment tracks of all time, Hill develops a thesis, a model, of what feminism and equality represents. In a call to all genders, Hill warns of the mistrust of others. She expresses the wisdom she learned from her prior relationships, relating to the listeners that her plight is relevant because she too is human.
>
> She reclaimed the necessity of not showing a difference in responsibility amongst the sexes, the blame both parties share in sympathizing with the gender roles imposed on young men and women. She earned my trust in that moment, no longer as the surrogate mother who sang me to sleep with a mother's tales I did not hear. With the love of an older sister, she earned my trust as a young woman.
>
> But what did I care about equality in gender roles? How did this affect a plucky teenager from rural Kentucky who still had an accent if she got pissed off? It didn't. It taught me about respecting myself. It taught me about valuing the respect of other people, which is something I never appreciated beforehand. And, as a barefoot baby from a house two hollers away from a Klan compound, it taught me that I didn't need a man, that I didn't need anyone. My nanny used to tell me to wear my rings like gypsies, proud, to show who I am. Hill said that, too, but from a perspective I needed to hear.

Ultimately, Victoria published the essay on her personal blog as a successful project. Even though she did not produce what she had originally proposed, her final essay was, as her peers had told her, the best thing she had written all year. In project-based writing, students can fail at what they set out to do and still be successful.

How to allow this degree of choice? (handwritten note)

"It only worked because it failed," Victoria texted me the night before she posted it online. This paradox is at the center of project-based writing. The personal lessons Victoria learned along the way about her ability to manage a project this large were almost as important as the writing itself.

A WORD ABOUT FAILURE AND THE EVOLUTION OF WRITING

In an interview on the occasion of his retirement from fiction writing, novelist Philip Roth said, "I no longer have the stamina to endure the frustration. Writing is frustration—it's daily frustration, not to mention humiliation. It's just like baseball: you fail two-thirds of the time" (Shteir 2014).

Failure, of course, in this context doesn't mean Roth failed as a writer or as a person, but that failure is inherent in the risk of writing and is a necessary component of the journey toward success and, ultimately, wisdom. Failure is the process by which novelists, essayists, social critics, screenwriters, journalists, and technical writers putter and noodle their way to the finished product.

In an interview with NEA's Rebecca Gross, novelist Toni Morrison (2014) said:

> As a writer, a failure is just information. It's something that I've done wrong in writing, or is inaccurate or unclear. I recognize failure—which is important; some people don't—and fix it, because it is data, it is information, knowledge of what does not work. That's rewriting and editing. . . . It's as though you're in a laboratory and you're working on an experiment with chemicals or with rats, and it doesn't work. It doesn't mix. You don't throw up your hands and run out of the lab. What you do is you identify the procedure and what went wrong and then correct it. If you think of [writing] simply as information, you can get closer to success.

This conceptual shift, looking at failure as data, is important. It's not the failure that makes a student a better writer; it's the identification of the failure as "just information" that can help them grow. This identification is the difference between students who see writing as a path of continuous growth and students who see writing as the result of a fixed point of ability, creativity, or talent. A smart English teacher will attempt to support student success and this grit-producing failure at the same time.

Yes, writing is incredibly, mind-bogglingly hard, but I would argue that teaching writers is even harder. A good high school English teacher attempts to create an environment wherein 150 students (with 150 sets of information and misinformation, memory, value, prejudice, vocabulary, and logic) grapple with the enormously complex tasks of (1) extracting the images and abstract thoughts from their subconscious, and (2) translating them into the best words in (3) the best order in (4) a cohesive form to (5) move an audience for (6) a specific purpose, using (7) appropriate-to-audience usage and grammar, and with (8) grace and beauty for all.

Gasp! That's a tall order.

And, in addition to this task, the good English teacher somehow needs to motivate students to continue doing this complex mission, wherein defeat figures prominently.

By employing the tenets of project-based writing, I could support failure in a way that taught the routines and tasks of successful failures, like Morrison and Roth, and provide support to students as they learned to see those failures as data for growth. This structure could not only be used to manage writing projects, but also as a system of management for any large project that was time and task dependent, in essence, everything in life.

I wanted to create a system where students could take risks as writers with subjects and forms without worrying about failing the assignment. Horrors. I wanted them to learn the habits of sustaining a project even when the end result of the project fell far short from their (or my) expectations. I also wanted them to develop resilience in the face of that failure, knowing they weren't getting dinged on their report card for taking risks that may have led to a failed writing product but paid enormous returns in other ways. *of course!*

But was Victoria's project a success? After all, she proposed to write a journalistic guide to hip-hop and she turned in a personal essay. In my class, there is a clear distinction between a student whose writing project evolves from an initial conception of one form into the final expression of another and a student who decides to cop out or drop out when the writing project becomes overwhelming. The cop-out/dropout student may propose a blog, but when she doesn't manage her time well or do the necessary research, she decides at the last minute to turn in five poems she wrote last summer. That's a cop-out/dropout, not an evolution.

Students can choose to cop out and drop out only one time in an academic year because this path doesn't teach them how to manage a project. One of my students, for example, was never satisfied with anything he wrote, so he would propose one thing and then at the last minute change his mind and turn in something short and half-baked. And often, he would claim to have been hijacked by a goon squad of muses: "But I couldn't help it; this novel just wants to be a vignette." In reality, he was battling two personal issues: a lack of respect for his own mind and the writing it produced, and an inability to manage his time.

Writing as evolution is different. Sometimes what we envision and what it turns out to be is something else entirely, but the core, the purpose, the force of the writing remains the same. Victoria wanted to write an homage to a type of music that held power and possession over her, and she thought the form for this love would be a journalistic guide, but when she started writing, she soon discovered the more appropriate fit for her true purpose was in the form of an essay. This is not a cop-out/dropout, but an evolution, which is encouraged and supported in the project-based writing classroom. This form-to-form evolution is another way students learn about their own learning, about how they think, and how that thinking becomes writing.

cop out vs. evolution

From a pedagogic standpoint, my gradual shift from traditional instruction to project-based learning was, in part, a growing awareness of how much I was depriving my students of this wisdom about their own identities as learners. I was cutting them out of the struggle of writing because I hadn't figured out a way to support the failure without failing the kid.

✗

RECOGNIZING STUDENT EXIGENCIES

In his book, *Between the World and Me*, Ta-Nehisi Coates (2015) says about his academic experience:

> I wanted to pursue things, to know things, but I could not match the
> means of knowing that came naturally to me with the expectations of
> professors. The pursuit of knowing was freedom to me, the right to
> declare your own curiosities and follow them in all manner of books. I
> was made for the library, not the classroom. The classroom was a jail of
> other people's interest. (48)

Good writing starts with a writer's own interest, grounded in her life and her observations about the world. Writing that originates in the mind of a teacher is, at best, an exercise, or more likely, as Coates says, "a jail." If we want better writing from our students, we must give them permission to declare their own curiosities and time and tools for "the pursuit of knowing."

Good writing—the writing we look to as models, for example, the Declaration of Independence, Lincoln's address at Gettysburg, Dr. King's letter from the Birmingham jail—is predicated on a great pressing need: the need to separate, the need to elegize, the need to explain. The only writing that will ever be valuable to a student will be that which comes from her own need to communicate, commiserate, or illuminate.

Our basic need to express anger, loneliness, torment, or joy will produce the best writing. Being assigned a topic, assigned a form, and assigned an audience undercuts the very human element that gives all writing its vibrancy.

In rhetoric, this pressing need is called *exigence*, defined as the circumstances that necessitate communication. All writing exists in this rhetorical situation between a writer, a reader, and the writer's need to communicate something. Writing without exigence is futile, exhausting to produce, and tedious to read.

Our job as teachers is to help students recognize their own exigencies as worthy and to examine them with utter seriousness. Writing about what you know is always good advice, but, more importantly, writing about what you care for is essential.

In my desire to teach informational, argumentative, and narrative models and provide students with organizers for their thoughts, I was circumventing the very thing that makes learning rewarding: wrestling with the unknown, sitting with ambiguity and uncertainty, and facing disappointment when the structure, for example, doesn't work. Figuring out what doesn't work is as valuable as figuring out what does work, but this process takes time, which teachers are always up against. What if, in the process of establishing their claim, students discover their original stance is indefensible, and they lose a whole day of research and writing? But isn't that what real writers do? Students may or may not succeed in writing the perfect argument or short story, but they are learning to value their own ideas, to manage their own time, and to set goals for themselves as learners and writers.

On Community:
The Key to Building a Project-Based Writing Classroom

ay one. Thirty students sit in your English II class. Some may be outright hostile, some suspicious, some hopefully polite. They're not in your class necessarily because they know you or chose you, but because English is a required class, and their poor beleaguered counselor had to find somewhere to put 2,000 kids during second period. Half of them were already over school by the fifth grade, but they're spiritedly chugging away at the game of public education.

The other half are a mélange of checked-out clock watchers or deliciously sarcastic gifted kids. A couple read grade levels below English II but have adult coping mechanisms. One is sick, a few are depressed, many are nervous. Your job is to teach them all. About how to read, how to write, how to understand language, how to communicate in groups and individually. How to be a compassionate human and a diligent citizen.

If I am to be an effective teacher, I must first change this harried, scattered culture and replace it with one of creative community. I know building community is the goal of every teacher, but that target is much more important in a project-based classroom because students are not just peers, but coartists and colaborers. They must trust each other and trust the teacher in her role to do this work.

Community is job number one, and the human connection forged in that environment, therefore, is the most vital component of any educational experience. Before students are willing to trot out their ideas, to become vulnerable to you and to other students, they first must sense that their voice, their self-knowledge, their world will be given serious consideration and will be fiercely protected from ridicule. The teacher in the project-based writing classroom must be skilled at breaking down barriers, engaging students with candor, and speaking to them with empathy.

To cultivate community, a teacher must also confirm the individual. Self-discovery, then, is job number two. Paradoxically, the way we create community is to recognize the opposite but equal singularity of all other humans in the room. The teacher must establish the primacy of each precious self and place its self-discovery at the center of his pedagogy. Writing and reading are the ultimate self-discovery indulgences, and English language arts, more so than any other discipline, asks us repeatedly to discover what it means to be alive.

In the natural world, learning is predicated on the self's need plus the self's desire. All authentic learning boils down to that. The smart teacher taps into the personal needs and desires of his students and rides that sap stream to teach the necessary skills to navigate life. If you choose to ignore community building and self-discovery as the cornerstones of your classroom, you're working against a billion-plus years of human development and culture. The master teacher activates and balances these two seemingly oppositional aims for the purposes of her own instructional goals and the advancement of her students.

START WITH STORY

In my classroom, we build community with stories. Big stories, little stories, told stories, written stories, happy stories, sad stories, scary stories, fantastical stories.

Tonight I'm watching the Tonys, wherein *Hamilton* has garnered eleven awards. The story, told through hip-hop by a culturally diverse cast about Alexander Hamilton, the first US treasury secretary, has made Broadway history. The musical's director, Thomas Kail, (2016) in his acceptance speech, said, "Let's continue to tell stories. There are still stories to be told, and there are people who want to hear them. Keep telling the stories."

From day one, I call my class a "writing community" or "writing studio," and our job is to produce, share, tell, and read stories. I tell them that writers in the world pay thousands of dollars to attend conferences or retreats to find other writers to create a safe, art-sustaining community in which to share their stories. This—I open my arms and swing about the room—is all spectacularly free.

"This class is special," I say. "We're going to write and say things in this class that you've never said or written in any other class yet in your high school career."

They may or may not buy that. It doesn't matter. You have announced the specialness of your intentions, you have piqued their interest, making outrageous claims. You must be crazy. At least this class won't be boring, they think.

"Good writing comes from the heart and the soul. We will not examine our hearts and souls lightly. We will examine them with gravity and kindness and clear eyes. We will write with a reverence for the act. And what we talk about in room 303 stays in room 303," I say.

Secrecy, hmm. Their eyes might light up a bit. They're not sold yet, of course. That comes later. But I have stated that our community exists to bolster each one of them in the heartbreaking, joyous act of unearthing and rendering life stories.

EMBRACE TRANSPARENCY

A great way to build a community that will support and bear witness to those stories is to tell your students exactly what's up from day one. Transparency is its own reward. They've been in classes where students had to "do" projects at the end of a teacher-directed unit, so it's imperative they understand your class is different. Tell them they get to choose their own writing topics and projects. Tell them you will provide them with a clear path for managing those projects from beginning to end. Tell them that although this kind of classroom works as a community, there will be large chunks of individual work time devoted to their projects, to meeting the expectations they set for themselves. Assure them their decisions about reading and writing will be independent, but not blind.

"I will help you find good stuff to read," I assure them.

"I'm intrigued," they will say.

"You should be," I say back.

Then I draw a giant mess on the board with paisleys and daggers and lightning bolts and stars and numbers and random words like *memory* and *values* and *language* and *that one time* and *cats*.

"This is what I carry around in my head," I say. "This is probably what you carry around in your head."

They nod, knowingly.

"How do you get this out of your head and get it on the page so that it makes sense and communicates something of value to another person?"

"A graphic organizer?" the yearner on the front row says.

"Voodoo," the smartie in the back row says.

"If I told you project management, would you turn me off?"

Some nod immediately.

"It sounds cold and sterile, right? Something you do at an office or a factory, not something you do in a writing class, right?"

Nods all around.

"What if I told you that project management is the way that real writers produce books and essays and screenplays? What if I told you Pixar used project management to produce *Toy Story* and J.J. Abrams used it to write *The Force Awakens*? And what if I told you project management is a way you could fail at writing, maybe even fail over and over while you figured out how to write, and you wouldn't fail this class?"

Eyebrows cocked. A few "what you say" side-eyes.

"We have thirty-six weeks in school. That's six nice tidy units of six weeks. Each six weeks, you get to pursue any project you would like, any topic, any genre, any length. I only set the final deadline for the project. All the other deadlines are up to you and the community of writers in this class."

Crickets.

"I'll help you find an idea that you want to write about, but it's up to you to be on the lookout for writing ideas. Writing ideas are everywhere. You probably encountered at least three this morning before school. Remember, it can be anything."

"Poetry?"

"Yes."

"A blog?"

"Yes."

"A screenplay?"

"Absolutely."

"On any topic?"

"Yes."

"Frog gigging?"

"That's one of my favorite topics."

"The deep web?"

"Of course. And once you've figured out a writing idea, you're going to pitch it to the class."

"Like a sales pitch?" Front row, again with all the answers.

"That's right. It's a lot like a sales pitch, except it's a writing idea pitch. The class will ask you questions about it, and then vote if they think you should write it."

"They're going to vote?"

"Yeah, but with kindness and cheering. There might be cupcakes involved. Remember, we're all in this together."

There's something about being completely transparent about the under-pinnings of your classroom that creates immediate buy-in with students. At the beginning of the year, I model a miniproject, and students select a small writing idea they would like to pursue. The purpose of this is to merely introduce them to the seven steps of the project-based writing flow, not for them to master it. That's what the rest of the year is for.

This is just to whet their appetite for what's to come.

CHAMPION THE UNIQUENESS OF YOUR APPROACH

Another element of creating community is to cultivate pride and ownership in the unique exclusivity of their work. One of the most remarkable things I've noticed about project-based learning classrooms is the way the students carry them-selves. They know that their class transcends the normal and has elevated itself into a unique stratum of high school existence. They become more professional, motivated, and self-possessed. Yes, they are still teenagers with all the weary ennui of their ilk, but, in project-based writing classrooms, they know they're part of something different, something greater, something not-school.

That tinder of specialness is the kindling on which to build the community fire. Although writers can write in any environment (Dostoyevsky + Siberian prison camp = *Crime and Punishment*) the environment of your classroom should signal to students they've left the brain freeze of institutionalized education far behind and entered into a different zone. The classroom should telepath: even though we are *in* school, we are not *of* school. The aesthetic says we are relaxed and fun, but productive, creative, and industrious. We are professionals with sincere and dreamy projects of our own. Is this the Brookings Institution? No, just English II, but very similar.

You must talk to your students as if they are already writers (which they are) even while you're asking them to become better than themselves. It's the "already/not yet" paradox that is paramount to building good relations with students. Believing they are already thinkers and writers forges the path on which they become better thinkers and writers. Treat their project ideas with the utmost seriousness, and they, in turn, will treat their projects and their work like authentic inventions. If she thinks I'm smart, maybe I should get busy being that.

My message is: yes, you get to chart your own course; yes, you have access to everything in this room. But having said that, serious business happens here. We enjoy this framework of freedom, and with freedom comes responsibility. We aren't sloppy, we don't goof off, do homework for other classes, or waste the time and space dedicated to our art. We are a community, and as such, we value our studio time, clean up after ourselves, and treat others with respect.

ESTABLISH A HAPPY COMMUNAL SPACE

Making your room bear little resemblance to a classroom is a good start. In a project-based learning classroom, the information is being created, manipulated, researched, analyzed, and re-created by each individual student. The classroom arrangement should mirror and support those activities. Although I'm explicit about the respect each student should give to the classroom environment and its occupants, I equally want them to feel comfortable and productive. The best description of my room came from one of my students who wrote that room 303 had "that local corner coffee shop vibe going, where you feel comfy and at home, but there's still the buzz of other working, living spirits in the room."

In essence, I want my high school classroom to be a cross between a scientific laboratory and a studio at a writing retreat. We have desks and tables around the room, but also armchairs, beanbags, pillows, and ottomans. There's a small library with rugs and couches for students who want to lounge as they write. Spaces for whole-group instruction, one-on-one conferencing, and small-group writing meetings are also present. I have an abundance of books and magazines on hand, a tech cart of laptops, and a giant tub of blank writing notebooks. I also have poster boards, index cards, and sticky notes for plotting. I keep a variety of art prints and photographs on hand if students need inspiration, and three giant boxes of writing prompts available to students who need a creative jump start.

physical space

I emphasize simple order to produce focus in the classroom because clutter leads to procrastination and despair. When you're finished, put things in their places. Make the room happy and fresh for the next class.

Do students occasionally abuse the classroom and its procedures? Of course. But students abuse the procedures of a traditional classroom as well, and, in fact, because a project-based classroom is predicated on student choice and student-directed decision making, I have fewer students abusing the system now than I did when I taught traditionally.

ROOT YOURSELF AS PART OF THE COMMUNITY

Another piece of the puzzle for community building is that you, the teacher, must be a participating, active member of this community. You're not just marching around the exterior, running maligners back into the village; you are a part of the village. And the best way to participate is to be a committed writer yourself.

I feel everything that needs to be said about the importance of English teachers to be active readers and writers has already been said by great teachers, like Nanci Atwell (1998), who taught me how to take the top of my head off in *In the Middle*, and Penny Kittle (2008), who, in *Write Beside Them*, seconds the necessity of making the machinery of your process available to your students. But even more than sharing the struggle and making your process transparent, writing with your students makes you humble in the face of the staggering, monumental task you are asking them to accomplish. Asking students to engage in the failure-tinged exercise of writing is a request that should not be made from the glib, satisfied stance of the academic or the critic. It must be made from someone who honors their struggle with a struggle of her own.

So if you're a writer right now, you're saying, "Check!" But if you're not a writer right now, you might be ready to flee. Don't go!

Could you write when your students write? When you're not conferencing with students, find a place on the floor, in a comfortable chair in the corner, or at a student desk and write, write, write. One or two days a week.

Could you write for ten minutes every morning before or after school? Whether you embark on a professional reflection journal or a gratitude journal or a poem a day, the practice will provide more insight to writing pedagogy than hundreds of hours of professional development. You would be well on your way to understanding many of the struggles your students experience.

What should you write about? If you don't know where to start, I love to use Pat Schneider's book *Writing Alone and With Others* (2003), which often helps when I teach adult writing classes. Schneider's approach is accessible and supportive, and she includes dozens of exercises for writing practice. Other great resources are three classics: Natalie Goldberg's (1986) *Writing Down the Bones*, Julie Cameron's (2002) *The Artist's Way*, and Anne Lamott's (1994) *Bird by Bird*.

Use our own writing process as PD

LAUNCH A SHARED NARRATIVE SPACE

The final piece of community building is to start talking to one another, preferably by becoming vulnerable and telling stories. During the first couple of days, I build community by telling stories about myself and allowing them to tell stories about their lives as well. I want them to meet each other in a <u>shared narrative space.</u> In addition to hitting nearly every core speaking and listening standard, these activities build community, and each time a student shares, I make mental notes about the stories they hold within them. These activities with storytelling at their base also reinforce narrative pacing, scene sequencing, detail selection, character development, and language usage.

During these activities, I'm learning a lot about my class, watching how they interact with one another. I'm looking for those who hang back, those who are leaders, those who are spitting fire, and those who have completely shrunk inside themselves.

There are some classes that need more or less community building than others. That's your call. I continue to build community throughout the year, but here are some activities I use as a starting place.

FIVE STORY-BASED COMMUNITY BUILDING ACTIVITIES

As someone who battles social anxiety, I recognize and sympathize with kids who hail from my awkward, introverted tribe. During the first few days of school, every teacher in every class is striving to get kids to interact with one another in an endless nightmare of icebreakers, such as trust falls and marshmallow-spaghetti activities. These goings-on stress me during professional development sessions, too.

When I employ these activities, I try to make them as low-stakes as possible. In other words, I don't want anyone to feel physically awkward, so the most extreme thing I might ask my students to do would be to sit in a circle with their peers or line up and face a partner.

Students need to talk to one another and interact, especially in a project-based writing classroom where their work will be dependent on and supported by their peers. But many times these getting-to-know-you activities are not connected in any meaningful way to the class itself. By framing these activities as a way for each student to discover potential writing ideas, the link to academic content somehow legitimizes the activity, so that they don't seem so excessively lame, and they shape into writing that will be pursued throughout the year. Because sharing stories early and often is an important gateway for generating writing projects later, I tie all activities to the very concrete instructional reality of writing and not to some intangible notion of breaking ice.

Tell Me a Story

One activity I love is called "Tell Me a Story." I ask students to form two lines of equal numbers and face each other, so each student starts out with a partner facing them. You could also do this with an inside-outside circle.

"I want you to introduce yourself to your partner and then tell them a story about something that really annoys you. The key is not just to say 'people who eat their boogers,' but to actually tell a story wherein people who eat their boogers figure prominently. You have two minutes. Talk!" I say.

After two minutes, I call time.

"OK, you've been telling stories about something that irritates you. Is everyone ticked off now?"

Whatever annoyance they've shared with their partner is a great place to start looking for a topic for a personal essay or a blog. Anything that raises your blood pressure is good writing coal, but I want them to start recognizing that even the simplest of things, like pet peeves, can make great writing projects.

"Do you think you could write about that? Maybe a rant, a manifesto, a screed?" Some students say yes, some look at me with "uh, no," and others just shrug. That's OK. I'm not asking them to write about it; I'm asking them to consider writing about it.

By asking them to consider everything as a possible writing idea, I'm asking them to start building a filter by which they see the world. In other words, frame everything they think, feel, do, observe, witness, or experience as a potential writing topic. Sometimes it doesn't occur to students that these aspects of their lives are actually worthy to be written about.

"Tell each other a story about something you are obsessed with," I say. For some reason this topic always gets them going. High schoolers are always obsessed with one thing or another, which is great. Good writers are obsessive types. After two minutes, I call time.

"Do you think you could write about your obsession?" Some of them say yes, others no, some still are just shrugging. That's OK. Not every prompt works for every kid.

My questions continue for as many rounds as we need: tell me a story about your favorite way to waste time; tell me a story about that person in your family that drives you teetotal crazy; tell me a story about the last time you were scared so badly you thought you were doing to die. And so on and so on.

I like to think of it as story speed dating for the perfect writing project.

Demographic Groups

Demographic grouping is an activity that asks kids to group themselves by various identities and meet the other people in the room who share that characteristic. As a group, I want them to share stories about what it's like to be a part of this subset of the larger population of kids at their school. They can also argue for or against their identity in this grouping.

I might ask them to group off by zodiac signs, for example. I will have printed off a generic description of a Taurus or Gemini or Pisces, and they form groups and then share stories in these groups as to how they are alike or unlike the description that is given in the horoscope. This is a great activity because it immediately creates kinship among disparate students in the class based on their birth month.

You can also do this activity with birth order. All the firstborn, middle, youngest, or only children get together in groups. I will have printed off descriptions of the characteristics of that particular birth order and the groups discuss whether they agree or disagree with the definition of their particular rank. Birth order is a great nugget of teacher information for me as well. I know firstborn kids are often my natural leaders, and when I select group leaders for inquiry sessions later in the year, this information will come in handy.

Another division I have used is the Myers-Briggs test, which students can take for free online, then group themselves according to personality type. I will have printed off the descriptions of the sixteen different personality types, and they will agree or disagree, in story, with the descriptions.

The key to doing this activity for both community building and self-discovery is to ask kids to argue for or against their own inclusion in this arbitrary demographic based on their life experiences, hence stories. They need to tell stories, trot out evidence, and qualify themselves as they talk, talk, talk and share, share, share about who they are or who they think they are.

7-11 Stories

This group sharing activity is based on the popular 21 Questions game, but oriented more toward generating narrative stories. It's called 7-11 because the storyteller has to include seven elements in his story and his audience has to ask eleven questions.

We sit in a circle on the floor, and I have a pot in the middle of the circle with about fifty generic nouns—pets, family, holidays, ocean, clubs, clothes, parties, shoes, hair, car, sports, food, friends, neighbors, and so on.

Someone draws a noun out of the hat, and she has to tell a story related to the noun with seven elements—place, time, characters, conflict, emotion, resolution, reflection. The story elements often tumble out in that order, but they don't have to.

Let's say a student picks out the card "neighbors." His story might run some-thing like, "Once when I was six [time] and we were living in a trailer park on the edge of Westerfield [place], my mom [character] got in a fight with the neighbor lady [character] about her goats coming over into our yard and eating all her tiger lilies [conflict]. My mom was screaming [emotion] and told her that if she didn't get those goats out of her yard, she was going to call the police. The neighbor lady then moved, but right before she moved, she mowed down Mom's tiger lilies for spite. [resolution] I'm glad we don't live there anymore [reflection].

That's it. Then the class asks the storyteller eleven questions. What kind of goats? Did she have any kids? Did your mom swear out a warrant and have her arrested for horticulture abuse? Where is Westerfield? What's it like to live in a trailer park? What did you do while your mom was yelling at the neighbor?

The questions are often the best part of this game because the storyteller recognizes that people are interested and willing to inquire for more information. The questions also help students recognize that a surface story can be deepened with rich details.

Never Have I Ever: Story Version

If you want to unleash students' most crazy stories and channel them into hysterical writing projects, look no further than the perennial slumber-party fave activity, Never Have I Ever . . . There are several ways to play this game, but we start with all students sitting in a circle holding up five fingers, then each person in the circle states a "Never have I ever . . ." statement.

For example, Trisha might say, "Never have I ever made a prank phone call." In the traditional game, anyone who has made a prank phone call must put one finger down and the game continues until you lose all your fingers, and you are out of the game. However, in our story version, someone who has made a prank phone call, for example, can tell their story of the prank phone call and earn the right to keep her finger up. If someone doesn't tell his story, his finger must go down. The winner of the game is the last person with any fingers left to give, so it's to their advantage to tell the stories and keep their fingers intact. This is a great activity that allows kids to get to know each other and to generate writing ideas. In fact, as we play this, I find myself asking them, "Hmm . . . is this a writing possibility?"

Two Truths and a Dream

Another great activity for ferreting out writing ideas and building community is a twist on the game Two Truths and a Lie, which is Two Truths and a Dream. Kids introduce themselves to the class using two facts that are true and one fact that is a dream of theirs. It's the job of the class to determine which are the truths and which is the dream. If students guess correctly, the person who introduced themselves must then tell the story of the origin of the dream. Tapping into their desires and dreams is a powerful first step toward getting in touch with their passions. Passions, obsessions, dreams: all of them are potential writing ideas.

A FINAL WORD ON COMMUNITY

Building community is one of the hardest things I do as a teacher, but it is the most lasting and the most valuable. In a small school, everyone already knows each other (and their mommas and cousins) and, like a giant dysfunctional family, they know what buttons to push to send each other right over the edge. In a large school, the kids may have never met each other, but they still may be harboring the wounds a high school hierarchy can deliver so sharply. Breaking down those barriers is a daunting task, but the efficacy of your classroom depends on it. It can be done. One of the closest, bravest, tightest writing communities I had the honor to teach was a group of forty freshmen and sophomores who were crammed into my little room during the last block of the day. In a school of 2,000 other students, they found each other. Writers need other writers. To tell the truth, to take risks, to be brave.

I always recommend Pat Schneider's *Writing Alone and With Others* (2003) to writers for the many writing exercises included, but her chapter on "Basic Principles of a Healthy Workshop" should be required reading for all writing teachers. In it, she lays out the guiding methods developed by the Amherst Writers & Artists in the late '70s for sustaining a community of writers. The five practices are a non-hierarchical spirit, confidentiality, balanced critique, cultivation of craft, and mutual trust. The five essential affirmations, which I teach explicitly to my students, are built on writing as "an art form available to all persons." The affirmations are:

1. Everyone has a strong, unique voice.

2. Everyone is born with creative genius.

3. Writing as an art form belongs to all people, regardless of economic class or educational level.

4. The teaching of craft can be done without damage to a writer's original voice or artistic self-esteem.

5. A writer is someone who writes (186).

From these five affirmations, the community can proceed as equal risk takers, assured of their place in my classroom. At the center of all functional communities is that sharing, and the shared property in my room is our stories. Our days begin and end with them. They are both the glue and the fuel for our purpose.

4

Discovering an Idea:
The First Step of Project-Based Writing

H elping kids discover an idea for a writing project is about helping them declare the truth. Not moralistic mumbo jumbo or Pinterest creeds, but truth telling with warts and scars exposed. Many students don't see their truths as substantive enough to write about, or they think writing ideas happen somewhere else, like outside their experiences. Asking them then to consider, maybe for the first time, their experiences as writing fodder is the initial step. And secondly, writers must have something to say about their experiences. There's nothing more relevant to a student than the opportunity to grapple with a topic born from his own existence in order to communicate it to another person.

Before we go any further into this chapter, let me ruminate for a moment on what I mean by discovering an idea. We urge students to find a "topic" for an argumentative or informational text or an "idea" for a narrative text, but neither of those terms is accurate or inclusive enough for what real writers do when they're inspired to write. Writers don't necessarily select a topic or an idea as much as they are gob-smacked by a character or a scene or an awareness of something significant in their own lives.

Without this initial awareness, students most likely have nothing to say. They may have a topic, but so what? They need an idea about the topic, which is to say, they must have had an epiphany about something in the form of a shock, a wonder, a revelation, an outrage. They must have the desire to communicate something, which is the exigent moment for all writing, including narratives. To investigate, to proclaim, to eulogize, to rage against, to declare. They must have, as educator Cheryl Glenn says in *The Harbrace Guide to Writing* (2012), "a real reason to send a message" (299).

In perhaps the most famous what-I-did-over-summer-vacation essay, E. B. White's "Once More to the Lake" (1992) isn't just about a trip to the lake, even though that's his topic—a trip he takes with his son to a lake in Maine, the same lake his father took him to when he was a boy. During the trip, he begins to feel as though he's living a "dual existence," that his son is really him and he is his father.

At what point did White get the idea to write an essay about his own mortality? Was it when they arrive at the lake and his mind returns "into the grooves which lead back"? Was it when the dragonfly lands on his fishing pole and convinces him "the years were a mirage and there had been no years"?

In the last sentence, White (spoiler alert) feels the "chill of death" in his own groin as his son pulls on a pair of wet swimming trunks. This moment completes several brushstrokes that build the power of this very human story, but it still may not have been the moment when White got the idea for this essay. Unless White has declared his moment of epiphany for this essay in a letter or interview I'm unaware of, we may never know when or how he got the idea. Perhaps he had a *Saturday Evening Post* deadline, and he was casting about for something to write, and it was actually *while* writing this little vacay ditty that he was thunderclapped by his mortal succession.

What we do know (and this is my point) is that regardless of when White got the idea to write about his own transience, the essay is a product of a mind open and aware to the significance of his experience. It was the written result of a writer poised, not just for ideas, but for the consciousness one can bring to that idea. An insight must strike a student first to write, and often the act of writing is where writers find the substance of their lives. Maybe White didn't even know until he was almost finished with his essay that it was about his own mortality. In this way, writing and discovering what one needs to write becomes almost a chicken-or-egg question, but the important point is that students need to be somewhere in the barnyard—thinking, writing, observing, noticing, open to the import of their lives.

So even though I'm using the term *idea* throughout this chapter, what I mean by *idea* is much more expansive than just a topic. It's the topic, yes, but it also includes the reason why the student has chosen this topic (the exigent need to speak) and, as Vivian Gornick (2001) says in *The Situation and the Story*, "the thing one has come to say" (36).

These moments are as true for writers of fiction as they are for writers of nonfiction. On his blog, Neil Gaiman (2011) posted an essay titled "Where Do You Get Your Ideas?" about this question he's often asked. His standard answer is, "I make them up. Out of my head." Which isn't the answer anyone is ever looking for. So when Gaiman spoke to his daughter's second-grade class, and one of her classmates asked him that question, Gaiman tried to do a little better.

"You get ideas from daydreaming. You get ideas from being bored. You get ideas all the time. The only difference between writers and other people is we notice when we're doing it."

Yes. The noticing. That's it. The awareness of one's own life.

The noticing, the recognizing, the skill of observing is the key to seeking and discovering ideas. It's a skill I want my students to develop. It's the practice, as former Kentucky poet laureate Frank X Walker described recently to a group of my students, of *looking* like a writer. Ideas are all around us—numerous, beautiful, bountiful ideas—but those who recognize these ideas as potential writing topics are those who are prepped for the catch. The key to developing ideas then is to train the brain to be the net.

CULTIVATE A PRACTICE OF NOTICING

From day one, I ask students to explicitly observe the world around them. Just as I mentioned in Chapter 3, I want my students to develop a "writing filter" that they apply to every experience they have. Ask students to listen to the way people talk. Ask them to compulsively record the events of their lives. Ask them to ask questions and entertain answers. Gaiman (2011) suggests that writers should continually wonder, "What if . . ." and "If only. . . ."

When students are asked to show up in the world with the critical tools of observation, collection, introspection, and creation, then every element in their lives suddenly becomes material for the next writing project.

Observing with a writer's eye and hearing with a writer's ear require practice. Something as simple as asking students to observe how people react to each other in an elevator or to observe how different social classes interact in the cafeteria is a step toward developing writerly sight. What moves any of us forward in the creative process is being engaged in the world around us—reading books and magazines, watching the news, movies, documentaries, talking to smart, interesting people, arguing with yourself and others.

Once they've noticed something in the world, students' observations may give rise to the need to communicate something. They might want to write a short story about two people trapped in an elevator as the world is ending or an essay analyzing the social divisions of a high school cafeteria. Both projects are solid. Both projects live or die on a student's ability to disclose his aims to his reader in an organized, artful manner with clear, purposeful language and then carry the project to its end. But the writing project is conceived by the writer first noticing something, then, assured of her ability to do so, telling it.

CULTIVATE A PRACTICE OF WRITING

After developing a practice of noticing, the primary activity that absolutely and directly impacts the development of a writer is, of course, writing. The act and practice of writing is the beginning of idea development in the project-based world. All the time. Any time. About anything and everything. Compulsive, constant chronicling and creating.

At the beginning of the year, my students and I have a discussion about writing as a skill that needs to be practiced regularly, just as the flutist flutes, the cooker cooks, and the baller balls. I tell them writing is a skill that develops both cognitively and kinesthetically over time. We also read Anne Lamott's "Shitty First Drafts" chapter from *Bird by Bird* (1994) where she advises writers to produce great quantities of writing, not necessarily quality, to tap into the good stuff.

Lamott says, "Almost all good writing begins with terrible first efforts. You need to start somewhere. Start by getting something—anything—down on paper" (32). I show them my own writing notebooks, starting with my first in 1982 when I was a freshman in high school to the one I'm carrying around in my purse. I explain that to write when I need to (a deadline), I write when I don't need to. I practice writing regularly without regard to censorship, prying eyes, public exposure, the voice of both internal and external critics.

Having considered all these things, I ask them to develop a writing practice, which meets three requirements:

- The practice is used for their growth as a writer.

- The practice must be exercised regularly.

- The practice must produce a quantity of writing over a period of time.

I give them a questionnaire (Figure 4.1) to assess their current writing practice as they reflect on the design of their writing practice contract (Figure 4.2). I want them to build both fluency and capacity for writing by writing.

Writing practice is independent of any project and is ongoing throughout the year. It is the place where most of their ideas will come from. I do not require a physical writing notebook as an assignment in my class, but I do require that each student cultivate an ongoing writing practice that is regularly documented and checked by me.

A writing practice embodies all the best and possible definitions of the term *practice:*

- Writing as the actual application of skill. (We are skilled in the *practice* of writing.)

- Writing as a habitual discipline. (We take our writing *practice* very seriously.)

- Writing as an activity to maintain and improve proficiency of skill. (I need to *practice* writing today to get better at it.)

The purpose of cultivating a writing practice is to develop a lifelong devotion to observation and self-chronicling. Serena, a recently graduated senior, wrote this in her reflection as part of her final exam:

> *I will keep a notebook until the day I die. The other day at work, I caught myself reaching for my notebook almost unconsciously to write something down, knowing full well that I would never turn it in for a grade ever again. I took this as a good sign. I always want to be the person who lunges for my notebook like it's an emergency EpiPen when I get throat-punched by a creative muse while going about my daily life.*

Within the first three weeks of school, I meet with each student and use the answers on their questionnaire to help them develop their writing practice contract (Figure 4.2). These contracts help students document and regulate their writing practice in a measurable way.

FIGURE 4.1

Writing Practice Questionnaire

 WE ARE WHAT WE REPEATEDLY DO. EXCELLENCE, THEN, IS NOT AN ACT, BUT A HABIT." – Aristotle

Writing is a skill that demands regular practice to improve. Similar to practicing tennis or piano scales, writing must be practiced regularly to build skill and strengthen proficiency. What writing habits do you already have? What habits can you develop to maintain a personal writing practice?

Answer the below questions to explore your present writing practice.

1. What time(s) of the day/week do you normally write?

2. In what physical space do you normally write?

3. On what material do you normally write (Google doc, iPhone app, notebook, Moleskin, etc.)?

4. What do you normally write about?

5. Do you share your writing with others?

6. If you share your writing with others, do you like feedback?

7. How many days out of a seven-day week do you engage in sustained writing?

8. When you engage in sustained writing, how long do you normally write (ten minutes, thirty minutes, one hour, etc.)?

9. Have you had periods of your life when you wrote more than others?

10. During those periods of writing, what conditions were present that made writing regularly easier?

FIGURE 4.2

Writing Practice Contract

Writing Practice Contract for _____

To improve my practice as a writer, I commit to the following goals:

From _____ to _____, I commit to writing (amount of writing or

amount of time) _____ daily or weekly (circle one) for a total of

(amount of total writing) _____ in my (record of

your practice) _____ due on _____.

Feedback?	
I would like Mrs. P to count my entries only but not read or respond.	
I would like Mrs. P to read my entries and only respond to the ones I've marked.	
I would like Mrs. P to read my entries and give me general holistic feedback.	
I would like Mrs. P to read my entries and give me feedback on each one.	

My Writing Practice Rubric	Excellent	Very Good	Good	Fair	Poor
Production of Writing Practice					

Signed (teacher) _____ Date _____

Signed (student) _____ Date _____

In the contract, students determine the parameters of both the "delivery method" of the writing (physical notebook, Evernote, Google Keep, Memo Note-pad, among others) and whether or not they want me to read and respond. Then we negotiate the amount of writing they feel would contribute to their growth as a writer (Figure 4.3).

FIGURE 4.3

Sampling of Student Writing Practice Contracts

	I commit to practice writing . . .	for this amount of time . . .	and/or . . .	for this amount of writing . . .	for a total of . . .	in this place of record . . .
K.F.	on Saturdays and Sundays at my house			500 words	6,000 words	Google doc in my Google Drive
E.S.	in the mornings before school starts	every morning		a single poem	30 poem drafts	my Moleskin
T.T.	every day in class during studio time	15 minutes			20 entries	my comp book
J.H.	two times a week, (maybe Mon & Fri?)			300 words on a 642 prompt*		Word doc in OneDrive
N.P.	after practice while I'm waiting on my dad (3× a week)	Usually it's about 15 minutes, but no more than 90			18 entries—I don't know the length	Evernote
M.H.	every B day			A full page	15 pages	my comp book
S.D.	at lunch on A days	10 minutes			15 entries	my journal
L.A.J.	two times a week during studio time			1,000 words	12,000 words	Word doc in OneDrive
J.M.	Mondays			½ a page on a question from the question deck†	6½ pages	my folder

continued

All students grow as writers using this contract, but not all contracts will produce the same amount of work—nor should they. I revisit these contracts three times in the year—once at the beginning, once in the middle of the year, and once at the end. The growth in the amount of writing and the amount of time spent writing is overwhelmingly evident. With each new contract, the student takes on a bit more challenging practice.

When students fill out the contract, they also create their own rubric based on their entries. They determine what an *excellent, very good, good, fair,* or *poor* writing practice would look like based on their stated goals.

I create a master list with student names and details of their contracts, so that I can easily assess their work each six weeks.

*This student is referencing the book 642 *Things to Write About* by the San Francisco Writers' Grotto, which we have in our classroom library.

†This student is referencing prompt decks I have in the room. These are decks of cards I buy cheaply and laminate a prompt on the face of the card. Each deck has fifty-two prompts, and I have the following decks: Write the Scene, Answer the Question, Finish the Sentence, Lift a Line, and Remember the Memory.

This contract allows students to develop a writing practice at their own pace, using their own goals and their own measurements for growth. Just as in a yoga class, not everyone will be doing forearm scorpion poses with abandon. Some of us hang out in downward dog for a year or two, but it's still a practice, and we will grow if we keep at it. The contract serves as a great tool for data collection to show writing fluency over time, and it's a gold mine for idea discovery.

TEN TOOLS FOR GENERATING IDEAS

In addition to asking students to become master observers of the world and to maintain a writing practice, I also lead them in specific activities early in the year that generate dozens of personal writing ideas.

Helping kids discover ideas at the beginning of the year and feeding that idea pot throughout the year is the key to a robust and healthy project-based environment. If students want good ideas for writing, they first must have A Lot of Ideas—some meh, some OK, some not bad, some heck yes! Students find ideas through all possible measures—art, music, conversation, movement, memory, dreams, visualization techniques, and arguments. I want my classroom to be a place of stimulation and connection, an epiphany bonfire.

I use the tried-and-true freewriting, listing, clustering, and webbing in my classroom, but here are a few others that hustle up ideas for students. The following activities can be used all at once at the beginning of the year or throughout the year to open each project cycle. One student wrote about her neighborhood and the crazy people in it all year long from the Neighborhood Map activity. Students pursued blog writing with ideas that surfaced during the Room for Debate exercise. Another student used ideas from his Life Inventory to create a poetry chapbook about his own identity as a young gay man in the South. Students return to the ideas generated by these activities over and over again.

THE WRITING WALKABOUT

The object of a writing walkabout is to walk and write, then walk and write some more. This is especially good for freshman or new kids, but it can be great for even upper classmen to see the school from a different angle. You leave the physical constraints of desks and chairs and fluorescent lights, and you go out into the world. (I learned about writing walkabouts from Richard Louth of the Southeastern Louisiana Writing Project when I attended a walkabout in New Orleans in 2003, and I've been using them ever since.)

As I take my class out for a writing walkabout, we walk for a while, then settle into a spot and write for fifteen or twenty minutes. Students can either describe what they see directly in front of them or describe what the place reminds them of. They can write from an exterior stance of description or from an interior stance of memory and nostalgia.

At Lafayette High School where I teach, I take my writing classes on a couple of walkabouts at the beginning of the year (Figure 4.4). Sometimes we walk around downtown or at our local cemetery, but I also take them on low-key walkabouts on school grounds: a little creek behind the school, the fifty-yard line of the football field, the sidewalk in front of the school, and outside our glass-windowed cafeteria. I'm always interested to see which students write about their own reflection in the glass and which students look past their reflection and describe the interior of the cafeteria. Every year I've done this, the class divides almost exactly down the middle in their approach to that glass window.

FIGURE 4.4

Writers on a Writing Walkabout

There's a poem in there somewhere, right?

When time is up at each space, students share what they've written with the person next to them. No real criticism or feedback is given. The space just absorbs the writing, and the group moves on to the next destination and repeats the process until the walkabout is finished. At the end of the walkabout, we return to the classroom, and I ask if anybody wants to share something they've written with the whole class. Even if we've only been together a few days, several students will volunteer. These volunteers are precious to the continued establishment of community. They become vulnerable and make it OK for another kid to find his voice and become vulnerable too.

THE FIRE PIT

One Friday four years ago, our school had an unusually long lockdown drill. We have these drills about once a month, and my class waits them out in a long, narrow closet that runs the length of my room. After my students hustled in and sat down, I turned off the light, and because the drill went on longer than normal, the kids started telling stories. The moment took on a summer-camp feel. We were sitting cross-legged in a small, tight circle in the dark.

There was 100 percent engagement around the circle. No sidebar conversations. No one checked cell phones. After one kid told a story, there would be laughter or questions or a small moment of lull, until another kid said, "Yeah that reminds me about once in fourth grade . . ." and we were off again.

"We should do this every Friday," somebody said.

Sitting around in a circle talking is not a new instructional technique. But it seems to happen less and less frequently. The demands of covering standards and integrating technology have crowded out the oldest curriculum trick in the world—tell a story, have a conversation, talk face-to-face with another human.

I use the Fire Pit every other Friday (Figure 4.5). I clear the desks out of the way, pitch my construction paper fire pit in the center of the room, and ask everyone to hunker down. At the beginning, you might have to tell a good story of your own or ask, "Anybody got a good school bathroom (or substitute teacher or bus ride or ghost) story?" These will start rolling, then build to a crescendo that only the bell will cut off.

FIGURE 4.5

Fire Pit

KOKOLOGY

When I was a sophomore in college, I took a psychology class, and in the text-book, there was a sidebar psychological quiz: imagine yourself journeying through a forest where you encounter trees, a cup, a key, a wall, and a bear. Each of these items represented a specific relationship. The trees represented parents, the cup represented love, the key represented money, and so on. I've always loved those kinds of parlor games, and during my first year of teaching, I decided to use it as an activity to teach metaphor and figurative language. It was wildly successful, and I've used it every year of my teaching career.

Two years ago, I stumbled upon a similar scenario game on the Internet, and as click led on to click, I discovered these games were an actual thing called "kokology." The word *kokology* is from the Japanese *kokoro,* meaning "mind, spirit, feelings," and from the Greek *logia,* meaning "the study of." In 2000, two Japanese psychologists, Tadahiko Nagao and Isamu Saito, published *Kokology: The Game of Self-Discovery*. A collection of these games were translated in 2000 and sold in the United States.

These game-based writing prompts are the ultimate in navel-gazing and funky fun times for the whole clan. Kids respond first in writing, then they share. The games—many are questions or scenarios—require students to answer questions or describe items that reveal the players' abstract attitudes about love, hate, envy, or pride. The classroom sharing out that ensues from this game is delicious, and the games generate dozens of writing ideas.

Many of the games have popped up as Buzzfeed quizzes online. I also use Evelyn McFarlane and James Saywell's *If... (Questions For The Game of Life)* (1995) and *How Far Will You Go? Questions to Test Your Limits* (1999), as well as Malcom Godwin's *Who Are You? 101 Ways of Seeing Yourself* (2000).

Life Inventory

When I was working as site coordinator for Rural Voices Radio, a National Writing Project program, I attended a workshop with poet Kim Stafford, the narrator for the thirteen-part radio series. He asked us a series of questions that related to our homes and our environment, such as "Where does your drinking water come from?" I got the idea that a similar inventory—asking students questions about their family, their culture, their faith, and their values—would be a great starting point for writing.

I developed 100 personal questions I've used every year. I ask students to answer each question with a declarative sentence, even if the answer is "I can't remember who . . ." or "I don't know why . . ." or "I don't care what . . ." Some years, I ask ten questions over the first ten days of school; other years, we go all in with the full 100 in a marathon writing session. The questions are divided into the old journalistic gleaning, 5Ws and 1H, and they run the gamut of "What gets you out of bed in the morning?" to "Where's the happiest place on earth?"

The key to completing the Life Inventory (Figure 4.6) is to use the answer to the question as an open door to walk into the room of a topic. Once you have a single declarative sentence, the door is open. Apply the 5Ws and the 1H to the opening sentence and keep writing. Look for or ascribe the significance of these moments.

For example, if a student answers, "My eighteen-month-old baby gets me out of bed in the morning," then that could be a great starting place for an essay about the struggles of parenting while in high school or the joys of being a single mom. It could also be the opening sentence in a short story about a fictional teen or a blog post about the morning routines of high school students who juggle school and parenting. The form and purpose develop as the significance reveals itself to the student.

FIGURE 4.6

Generative Exercise: Life Inventory

Instructions: Answer each question with a complete sentence. Answer each question with the first thing that pops into your head. Answer each question honestly. After answering all 100 questions, review your answers and circle three sentences that are interesting, compelling, startling, or surprising. Share your three sentences with a small group. Choose one sentence you are the most interested in writing about and copy it at the top of a blank sheet of paper. Write for twenty minutes without stopping, starting with this single sentence.

continued

WHO

1. Who, in your family, are you most like?

2. Who scares you?

3. Who wrote your favorite book?

4. Who's the most creative person that you know?

5. Who makes you laugh the most?

6. Who first taught you about love?

7. Who gave you your first job?

8. Who was the first dead person you saw?

9. Who's the last person you shared a secret with?

10. Who truly gets you?

11. Who keeps the monsters away?

12. Who would not be happy for you if you won the lottery tonight?

13. Who defends you?

14. Who do you run to when you're scared?

15. Who is your best friend?

16. Whose hand do you want to be holding when you die?

17. Who makes you nervous?

18. Who would you like to run away with?

19. Who, in your friend group, will be the one who is most likely to succeed?

20. Who is the last person you lied to?

continued

WHAT

1. What gets you out of bed in the morning?

2. What is the name of the street you grew up on?

3. What's the most difficult subject you've ever tried to learn?

4. What do you fear the most?

5. What is your favorite food?

6. What's your favorite memory?

7. What's the first book you remember reading?

8. What did you dream about last night?

9. What one word characterizes you?

10. What is the name of your future child?

11. What do you believe is true even though you cannot prove it?

12. What was the biggest mistake you've ever made?

13. What is the hardest lesson you've ever learned?

14. What was the bravest thing you've ever done?

15. What is the title of the movie of your life?

16. What makes you mad?

17. What is the last thing you think about at night before you fall asleep?

18. What is your favorite question?

19. What doesn't make sense to you about the world?

20. What will happen tomorrow?

continued

WHERE

1. Where were you born?

2. Where's your favorite vacation spot?

3. Where do you like to hide?

4. Where did you go to elementary school?

5. Where would you go in a time machine?

6. Where were you last night?

7. Where do you go to think?

8. Where did you get your nose?

9. Where is the saddest place you've ever been?

10. Where does your love live?

11. Where does your drinking water come from?

12. Where does your god live?

13. Where do you go to have a good time?

14. Where do you watch the sun set?

15. Where is the safest place in your house?

16. Where is your birth certificate?

17. Where's the strangest place you've ever been?

18. Where is the happiest place on earth?

19. Where will you live when you are fifty?

20. Where do the spirits of the dead go?

continued

WHEN

1. When was the first time you rode in a plane?

2. When was the first time you realized your parents were human?

3. When did you lose faith in someone?

4. When did you lose something you cherished?

5. When will you be good enough?

6. When did you meet your best friend?

7. When did you ever fear for your own life?

8. When did you finally understand the truth about yourself?

9. When did you fall in love?

10. When did you first realize people betray each other?

11. When did you feel the most loved?

12. When did you learn to whistle?

13. When did you cook your first meal?

14. When have you ever done something illegal?

15. When did you accept yourself?

16. When have you had enough?

17. When was the last time you broke a promise?

18. When will your dreams become reality?

19. When do you think you will die?

20. When was the last time you were sick?

continued

WHY/HOW

1. Why are you here?

2. Why do you live where you live?

3. Why can't all people live in peace?

4. Why do you care?

5. Why do you still hope?

6. Why did the chicken cross the road?

7. Why do you gossip?

8. Why are you the person you are?

9. Why are you the gender you are?

10. Why does life end?

11. How do you like your eggs?

12. How does betrayal feel?

13. How do you pray?

14. How does it feel to be in control?

15. How do you motivate yourself?

16. How do you lie to yourself?

17. How do you know if someone is lying to you?

18. How do you dance?

19. How do you want to improve yourself?

20. How will the world end?

Story-Place Maps

Another activity I have adapted is from Bill Roorbach's *Writing Life Stories* (2008) called Neighborhood Maps (86). I widen the possibilities a bit and include any place where stories live. Maps of any kind (life, love, fashion, literacy, school) are a great way to generate ideas for writing. Check out Georgia Heard's *Heart Maps* (2016) for other great map exercises. Allowing students to visually connect time and place to the stories embedded in that place is a powerful resurrection tool.

Students draw a map of any place on a piece of poster board. It might be a subdivision, a rural road, an apartment complex, a farm, or even a house. I've even had some kids draw a map of the inside of their heads, a map of their future space colony, and a house that existed only in their dreams. I don't really care what place they choose as long as they draw it exhaustively—streets, houses, fire departments, bodegas, mosques, vacant lots, office buildings, junkyards, plains—and exhume the stories nestled inside.

Once they've drawn the map, I ask them to label all the features of the map with names, such as "Ascension Episcopal Church" or "51st Street." If they don't remember the names of the people who lived in certain houses, they can write labels such as "mean old woman with a six-foot iguana."

Then I give them sticky colored dots, although you could also use mini-sticky notes, and ask them to remember all the things that happened in that place. I tell them to put a story dot or sticky note near the spot where a memory lives and write a few lines about that memory. For example, they might write "tree I fell out of and broke my arm," or "where I hide to get away from my sister." The more memories they stake out, the better. Events that didn't happen to them, but were known to have happened in that space, should also be included. I've also done this activity with three transparency sheets. Students draw the map on one sheet, then layer another sheet on top and write all the labels, then layer the other transparency on top of that and write all the stories on the third sheet.

Once everyone has a map littered with story dots, we break out into groups, and students take their group on a guided tour throughout their place. The group asks each other questions about the map and the stories involved. Once sharing is over, writers choose one story from the map or one story that surfaced from the map to write. The story the writer is most anxious to write or the story about which the group showed the most interest are two good bets.

This activity draws the memories out first through a drawing, then labeling, then story gathering, then through sharing with another person. By the time the writer goes through all four steps, she'll be ready to write one of the emerging stories with lots of sensory details and specific memories. The map is also one of those generative exercises students can return to again and again to develop even a series of place-based projects, similar to Cisneros' vignettes in *The House on Mango Street* (1991).

Family Story Tree and Family Isn't Always Blood Story Tree

Similar to the place map, a Family Story Tree is a great way to mine the inherited stories, tales, and language from one's own family. In communities where an oral tradition is still vibrant, this activity renders dozens of great personal writing ideas. Students draw a family tree on a poster board. This can be a traditional tree or some other kind of living visual—a giant shrub, a puffy topiary, or a lanky espalier. Once the tree is drawn and the names affixed to the branches, I tell students to censor nothing and to commit all stories, descriptions, memories, even bits of dialogue on the tree next to the family member's name.

Several years ago, a student asked if she could put some people on her family tree who were not family. Most high school students identify and value those people who are in their life by choice, not by blood. Of course, I said, and from that point forward, I've encouraged students to draw as many story trees as necessary to accommodate any social and culture groups to which they belong. Some students make story trees for different friend and family groups at different times in their lives—a biological family tree and blended family tree, a neighborhood friends tree and a school friends tree, or a middle school friends tree and a high school friends tree.

The key to this activity is the same as the Neighborhood Map and the Life Inventory. Generating these ideas through the peoplescape of life is another open door into a room full of topics. Each limb of the topiary can represent a writing project—a reflection, an argument, a blog post, a personal narrative, or an informational text. Perhaps in drawing and transcribing a story tree a student might also discover some larger abstract theme or purpose about her identity in this group. And when that happens, a student's writing project life is sealed. She can write on that topic all year long in various forms and for various purposes.

This I Believe

This I Believe has been a staple in my writing classroom for decades. Both confident and reluctant writers respond to these short, from-the-heart statements of personal belief with "this-I-believe" moments of their own.

Based on a radio program in the '50s hosted by Edward R. Murrow, *This I Believe* was a feature on National Public Radio for many years, and essays can now be heard on a weekly podcast at http://thisibelieve.org/podcasts/. Along with several book collections, including my favorite regional, *This I Believe: Kentucky* (Gediman 2013), the *This I Believe* program hosts a fantastic collection of 500- to 600-word essay models about personal philosophies with subjects as diverse as addiction, science, spirituality, community, pets, social justice, war, or work.

Formulation of identity and the negotiations of independence in teens often throws the values and beliefs with which they've grown up into flux. This activity asks students to honor and recognize the beliefs that brought them up while also recognizing the evolution of their worldview as they become more critically aware and autonomous as humans. Asking students to write about their personal beliefs is a powerful exercise, specifically when you ask them why these values are important to them and what stories from their life have contributed to their credo.

Before we read any model essays, I lead students in a values activity to generate several belief statements and stories from their life that supports these values. I give each student five index cards. On one side of each card, students write a belief statement, such as "I believe nothing good ever lasts," and on the other side of the card, I ask them to jot down a story from their lives that supports or explains why they believe that. I then read the original invitation (1954) to *This I Believe* contributors to my students:

> *You must write it yourself, in the language most natural to you. We ask you to write in your own words and then record in your own voice. You may even find that it takes a request like this for you to reveal some of your own beliefs to yourself.*
>
> . . .
>
> *We do not want a sermon, religious or lay; we do not want editorializing or sectarianism or "finger-pointing." We do not even want your views on the American way of life, or democracy or free enterprise. These are important but for another occasion. We want to know what you live by.*

After reading this eloquent invitation, I ask students to choose one of the five belief statements, the one that most closely aligns with what they perceive as their credo or core value, and we freewrite for twenty minutes or so. I ask students to put it away and forget about it, but the next day, I ask them to pull it back out again and add something more to their freewrite. I might do this layering activity five days in a row. Or ten. Or twenty. Each day a new layer is added until students have a lot of material if they want to pursue this idea as a writing project.

Students can also browse thousands of *This I Believe* essays online, which are grouped under seventy-five different topical themes. Students can select three or four essays on a similar topic, then freewrite about that topic from their own personal stance. There is also a cache of essays written by students eighteen years or younger at https://thisibelieve.org/essays/age/under18/ that students can use as models for writing about their personal philosophies.

Personal Universe Deck

Personal Universe Deck is a great way to tap into kids' linguistic whimsy and their sense of playfulness with words. Plus kids get a personal deck of 100 word cards they can keep all year long or for the rest of their lives. The Personal Universe Deck as a writing exercise has been attributed to American poet and playwright Michael McClure. (You can listen to the original lesson (1976), which is a delight, on the JKS Audio Collection at the Naropa University Archives: http://cdm16621. contentdm.oclc.org/cdm/ref/collection/p16621coll1/id/1491.) I have tweaked and adapted this activity many times to teach a host of writing and language skills.

First I ask kids to write 100 concrete, specific words that represent their individual, personal, beautiful universe. The words need to be words each kid loves, words she thinks are beautiful and exemplifies who she is, and words that are in some way associated with the five senses. The words should also represent the student's past, present, and future, both positively and negatively.

I model this on the board: "OK, start with free association on a clean sheet of paper. Start with the first word that occurs to you. *Lilac.* I don't know why I just thought of that, but my grandmother had lilac bushes in her yard, and I'm trying to keep in mind my past, present, future. Each word needs to have some significance to you, so *lilac.* That's a smell word, right? And now I'm standing in my grandmother's yard by the lilac bush, and do I hear anything? How about thunder? Sure.

I visited her in the summers, and storms popped up a lot. That would be a sound for me. Now, just start associating. Hmm, my grandfather's dairy barn. *Barn* is one of my words. That might be a touch word for me because I remember the cold smooth concrete of the barn walls."

The next day, we create another 100 words. I would go through the same modeling on the board with my own life to generate 100 more words. My philosophy is that each kid needs 200 to 300 words to find the best 100 words that represent his life.

On the third day, students start weeding and whittling down their words to the essential 100. I remind them the words should not be descriptive of senses, like *salty* or *sweet*, but concrete words like *hot dog* or *custard*. I tell them to cut out the vague words and replace them with specific. Avoid *bird*; instead say *wren* or *raven* or *blue jay*. Also, cut out words with suffixes, like *-ing, -ly, -ed, -s*.

On the fourth day, students start selecting words for categories. Eighty of the words need to be related to the five senses: sixteen words for sight, sixteen words for sound, sixteen words for smell, sixteen words for touch, sixteen words for taste. Then they add ten words for *movement*, then add three words for *abstraction*. Then the last seven words are anything else they want. Kids can make a chart like the one below in their writing practice for classification, or just number their words.

SIGHT	SMELL	SOUNDS	TASTE
16 words	16 words	16 words	16 words
TOUCH	MOVEMENT	ABSTRACTION	ANYTHING
16 words	10 words	3 words	7 words

On the last day, I give each kid fifty index cards, and they fold and cut them in half into 100 small cards that create their "deck." On the back of the card, they can write their initials or some tag that indicates the card is theirs. On the front of the card, they write one glorious word. Repeat ninety-nine times. Presto, their own Personal Universe Deck! (You can even get fancy and laminate these if you bring your media technician a nice pie and promise to clean her house.)

Kids use their Personal Universe Decks for writing poetry, memoir, short fiction, and argument. Sometimes I ask each student to throw three cards into a basket, then I pull out ten cards, write the words on the board, and we write a short informational text or narrative based on the words. You can return to this deck over and over throughout the year for great impromptu writings.

Observation Logs

Observation logs are pocket-size notebooks that students stick in their pockets and whip out every single time they see, hear, touch, taste, smell, or feel something. The point is simple: develop a habit of noticing things and writing them down.

In 2009, my AP Language class read Joan Didion's (2008) masterpiece essay "On Keeping a Notebook" and were duly inspired to take up pen and paper and practice the art of observation. This activity is refreshingly simple. Teaching students to observe their world with no other objective than merely witnessing it is absolutely vital.

Didion says, "We forget all too soon the things we thought we could never forget. We forget the loves and the betrayals alike, forget what we whispered and what we screamed, forget who we were. I have already lost touch with a couple of people I used to be" (76).

I want them to cultivate a writerly habit that some of my students already have: compulsive recording. But even more important than the chronicling itself is the action that comes before the chronicling: the noticing. Everything becomes a rich opportunity.

"But what do we write?" someone always asks. And I answer . . .

phrases that tickle your fancy	riddles	wishes you had at five
geography phrases	lies	wishes you had last year
grandma phrases	mysteries	wishes you have now
sister phrases	tall tales	hurtful disappointments

continued

temple phrases	visions	happy inspirations
notes from a lecture	memes	fears you project
notes from a talk show	quotes	fears you hide
underground notes	revelations	scientific discoveries
gossip you hear	secrets	scientific hypotheses
gossip you make up	graffiti	lists of things you carry
news	Facebook updates	asleep dreams
sermons	Twitter shout-outs	woke dreams
songs	a wedding toast	new words you learn
headlines	a funeral prayer	new words you make up
lists	a speech you hear	an old word you forgot
jokes	a scene you see	names of friends
	a scene you make up	

Room for Debate

To get students thinking critically about current events, I write an essential question on the board: Does a political candidate's religion matter? Are news outlets biased? Should drug addicts be forced into rehab? Students then scribble down their thoughts for five minutes, after which they read a short article about the same topic from *The New York Times'* fantastic resource Room for Debate, a topical collection of short articles from all sides of each issue. After reading, students break out into small groups to unpack their articles, then we finally convene for a quick group discussion. The whole process takes about twenty to thirty minutes of a ninety-minute instructional block.

The majority of writing projects that come from the Room for Debate activities end up as blog posts arguments, but students always walk away from these activities with writing ideas, primarily because the topics are contemporary, relevant to their lives, and controversial.

JUST PICK ONE ALREADY

So that's it! At the beginning of the year, I use these prompts to get the wheels turning, but students can take them or leave them. When I first introduced the idea of project-based writing, some students were hesitant (Is this a trick?), some students were resistant (Why do you hate me?), while some students were overjoyed (Free at last!). Just giving kids the freedom to choose their own topics is the first step, but giving them freedom doesn't necessarily mean they will recognize and capitalize on an idea they want to write about.

Some kids immediately know what they want to write, but others are more like many of us who stand in front of a pantry full of food and exclaim, "There's nothing to eat in this house!" Of course, there's always canned tuna, evaporated milk, and a tin of stale cookies you bought from a band fundraiser, but none of that sounds appealing. Same for kids with twenty pages of writing ideas. "But I don't like any of them!" they whine. You want them to look for the spark, the epiphany, the revelation about the topic that brings them to the message they need or want to speak.

At this point, I will step in and inquire with prods and pokes.

- What writing idea has the most energy?
- What writing idea produces the most emotion, either positive or negative, in you?
- If you had exactly one week left to live and you could write only one thing, what would you write?
- What is a piece of writing that you would like to read?
- Is there an idea in your notebook that seems to be begging you to write about it?
- Is there a writing idea that would work as an assignment for another class? (I encourage this kind of double-dipping, and sometimes well-crafted assignments can provide exigence in motivated students.)

- Do you respect your own mind? Are none of your ideas appealing to you because they are your ideas and not someone else's? (The answer to this question may necessitate further conversations about nonwriting insecurities. I recommend Ralph Keyes' book [1995] *The Courage to Write* to many students whose anxiety sabotages their best intentions.)

Here's another trick if students still can't hammer down a writing idea. Out of the fifty or 100 writing ideas they've generated in their writing practices, I ask students to write five on a sheet of paper, then give me the paper. I randomly circle one of the ideas and hand it back to them.

"There. Write about this." If they enthusiastically say, "Yes, yes, that's the one I was thinking about," then we've got a winner. But if their face turns the color of chalk and their lip droops, I know they really needed to write about another topic on the list.

"Which is it then?" I ask. And they point to the one of the list that they most want to write about. Look at that! The heart always bears out its topic.

Of course, once a student has a writing idea, it's not a "project" yet, but the process of prepitch, pitch, and proposal, which we will discuss in the next chapter, will begin to add some heft to the idea. Right now it's just a zygote in the eye of the writer. My student Colin wrote in his notebook, "I have a character in my head called Erastus, but other than his name I don't have any idea what his story is, but I want to know."

This is how writing starts. Just a name. Just a memory. Just a feeling.

And all writing then proceeds as a riddle with no setup, a puzzle with no picture, a math problem without numbers, all of it invented as it's being invented, solved as it's being resolved and solved again.

So how do you move students from exigent little baby ideas into full-blown writing projects? It requires more discovery and exploring, but also some definite steps toward framing the idea with pitches and proposals.

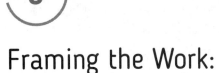

5

Framing the Work:
Developing a Pitch and Proposal

Once a student has settled on an idea, he starts to frame it into a project. The first steps on this path are developing a pitch and writing a proposal.

Just as I defined "idea" in Chapter 4, let me also define a "writing project." Whereas the term *idea* encompasses a lot more than just an idea (epiphany, message, purpose, topic), the term *writing project* also encompasses multiple things, but specifically the act of writing and the production of an artifact of text over time. The project of writing is the original idea married to the work of writing bound by real time and real-world considerations of word counts, deadlines, and submission guidelines.

Here's an example: I'm a freelance writer who regularly pitches article ideas to regional magazines. When the Commonwealth of Kentucky recently increased the value of tax credits for producers making films in our state, I had an idea that this would make a great feature article, specifically looking at the economic impact of an LA production company filming in the small town of Springfield, population 2,519. At this point, I just had an idea. However, once I pitched the idea to the editorial board at a regional magazine, and they got interested, the idea became a project because it was then tied to a specific audience with certain time and word count expectations.

The project, then, encompasses all the mental and physical work that brings this idea into the world as a deliverable piece of text: the pitch, the query, the creation and maintenance of a source list, the preinterview research, the interview transcriptions, the content research, the drafting, organizing, revising, and the final fact-checking, plus keeping it under my word count limit and delivering it to my editor before the deadline.

This project, however, looks or feels nothing like the novel I'm working on. I have no editor waiting on that, no requested word count, no deadlines except the ones I have imposed upon my process to produce this work. In so doing, I try to deliver one chapter a month to my writing group, which meets monthly at my house. I've finished exactly three chapters, which is to say, I've rewritten the same chapter three times because I haven't figured out how to tell the story I want to tell. Obviously, this writing project operates very differently than my freelance work.

And that project looks nothing like the assignments I had to do in graduate school, or the series of letters I wrote to my mother when I left home at eighteen, or the blogs I write concerning teaching.

But all of those are writing projects. The project is not a single action or even a single process, but a mixture of actions and processes and procedures bound by time and the desire to deliver a finished product, which will presumably be read or watched by an audience. In this way, teaching students the specific path and tools of project management, from originating to planning to executing, helps them become better writers because it helps them manage the project of writing as they become better at the act of writing itself.

Let me stop here a moment and digress even further to address the creative writers who are rolling around on the floor stifling screams. For many poets and writers, planning negates art. For fiction writers, in particular, talking about the writing instead of actually writing is to replace a roaring fire with a tiny flaming candle. I get it.

In Ron Carlson's (2007) brilliant little book, *Ron Carlson Writes a Story*, he says, "Much of a writer's work is exploration, and that involves so many things he cannot know from the outside" (16). I completely agree with this, but protecting the explorative spark of art doesn't impede the proposal process or vice versa. All writing can benefit from some preliminary planning, as long as that planning serves to support the evolving project and not bind it into some compositional straitjacket.

Framing an idea is an extended invitation to think about what will be written and why it should be written. For reluctant and developing student writers, the framing process is an opportunity to explore and create and think. The universe and their imaginations will still have many mysteries to unfold when they begin to write the actual piece.

The first step of this framing is giving a pitch and writing a proposal. Pitching and proposing a writing project puts a kid out there in a way no teacher-generated assignment will ever do. The pronouncement of a student's writing plan creates anticipation in other students, and the framing process taps into the best kind of peer pressure because it creates an immediate audience. A waiting, cheering, real audience.

There's also something magical about practicing a pitch and writing a proposal as a way to think through an idea. It's the first of many opportunities students will have in this cycle to write about the idea they'll eventually end up writing as a product. As one student, Joe, said about the process, "With the pitch and proposal it kind of makes you as the writer actually think about what you'll be writing. Because before the pitch it's a lot of times just 'I have this idea' and what the pitch does to me at least is it makes me think about what this thing will look like. It kind of gets you sweating and motivates you to start working so you don't look like a fool."

HOW DO STUDENTS PITCH?

The main objective of pitching is to increase a student's ability to articulate, in a clear, succinct manner, his idea, but the secondary joys of pitching are myriad. Students develop their own speaking and listening skills when they pitch, and as they listen to others pitch and give feedback, the whole process develops community and increases the intellectual capital in the room.

The pitch is based on the widely practiced art of elevator pitches. Different than a sales pitch, which is more of a formal presentation, the elevator pitch is a conversation starter. The pitch needs to be brief, easy to understand, and interesting.

For every project cycle, I devote an entire week to pitches because I want to support this important process as much as I can. During Pitch Week, students work in prepitching groups for two days, and the remaining three days are devoted to pitching.

PREPITCH

Some students arrive at prepitch with a vague, nebulous idea, but during this process of inquiry, they often zero in on the form or genre they think would best deliver the idea they want to write about. During the two days of prepitch, I encourage students to toss their ideas around in a smaller subwriting group inside the larger community. These small writing groups can shift and change and transform with each project cycle. Most of the time, the groups are student selected, but occasionally, I group kids who are writing narratives together, kids who are writing blogs together, kids writing poetry in a poetry squad, and so on.

If you are requiring students to write in a specific genre, they can still choose their own topics and pitch their ideas as a way to think through possibilities before writing. Just tweak the questions you ask students to think about to match the decisions you're allowing them to make. The question "Why are you writing this?," for example, might become, "Why are you interested in this topic?"

No one writes anything down in this process; the currency is conversation and inquiry, juggling and spinning ideas verbally. Each group works through five prepitch questions, which are adapted from project management consultant Michael Dobson's book *Creative Project Management* (2010).

What do you want to write about?

This is the first time the student will be required to verbally explain what he wants to write about for this project. This is a great time for hemming and hawing, and the struggle is very real. Students may have four or five things they want to write about and want feedback from their group. They may have nothing they want to write about, and the group can help them discover a potential project because they have all, during class exercises, generated writing about people, places, neighborhoods, current events, memories, values, beliefs, and philosophy. The options are wide open, which is why this step is so difficult and so important. Students will struggle here, but there's group support as well as zero risk. You can try on any outfit in the prepitch to see if it fits.

Why are you writing this?

This is the most essential question of the five. Why is this character, scene, idea, position, memory important to you? Students that demonstrate passion and curiosity demonstrate the necessary energy that will see the piece through to completion. Students who are wishy-washy about their project or are only marginally interested in it are encouraged to hunt more deeply for purpose. I have a lot of conferences during these two days with students to help them tease out the topic they really want and need to write if the writing groups haven't helped them.

Who would be interested in reading this?

This question tells me if the student has thought about the world in relation to his idea. Sometimes I ask, "Who do you want to hear this message?" This question aims at audience awareness. The person or persons to whom and for whom a writer writes will help a student figure out the appropriate tone and voice. If a student knows he wants to write a satirical essay on cliques for the high school newspaper, he will also understand what will appeal to this audience, what examples, illustrations, and words will most likely move this audience. If a student wants to write a mockumentary for his YouTube followers, that will be a different audience altogether even though those two audiences may be occupied by many of the same people. Imagining the readership for the message a student wants to send or the story he wants to tell is a necessary component of prepitch.

Why are you the person to write this?

This question is important because students may not see their own unique perspective as being a contributing factor to the success of a writing project. Again, if they have been writing "for school" and not for themselves, they may not know why they are the person to write this. This is also an opportunity for me to reinforce the uniqueness of their voice in a cacophony of voices who have written about this subject or this form before. I remind them all plots have been written, all arguments have been made, but not by *them*. As a plotline, the quest is as old as humanity, but we still want to hear George Lucas' version in *Star Wars*, which is different from Speilberg's take in *Raiders of the Lost Ark,* which is even different from the quest in *The Wizard of Oz*. The intersection with the age-old plot or argument and their lives, their childhoods, backgrounds, belief systems gives rise to originality and creativity.

What form will this idea take?

Would a student's idea that his school needs more nutritious school lunches be better served up as a blog post or as a letter to the principal? What will best memorialize Saturday morning fishing trips with a grandfather? Is it a poem or a letter to him? What genre or form will best explain what it feels like to lose your best friend when she suddenly has a boyfriend? Is it a personal narrative, a short story, an essay about friendship? This question begins to marry the project to an outside audience. Having a real audience—not just the teacher or students—is absolutely essential in any kind of project-based learning. Shaping an idea into the frame of a purpose—to inform, to celebrate, to persuade and so on—and coupling it with a known form, like an essay or a short story or a blog, is the first step toward thinking about audience.

Now, you might be thinking, "Without explicitly teaching purpose and form, how will my students know what is available to them?" When it comes to selecting a purpose or form, I believe the idea itself springs from its own purpose and that idea will select its own form. I ascribe to the architectural principle that form follows function, or the way something is presented to the world (its form) is determined by its purpose (its function).

Scarlett's brother was murdered, and she wants to write about him, but in what way? How? Once she determines her purpose, her form will follow. Is her purpose to argue for stricter gun laws? Maybe an argumentative blog post or letter to her state representative. Is her purpose to elegize him? Maybe a personal essay about his life. To memorialize? Maybe a collection of poems or a series of vignettes. Maybe she doesn't even know what she wants to say about the passing of her brother, and in the writing, she discovers a form.

Students must discover, just as real writers do, the purposes and forms their ideas will take. Any form of writing they know exists in the world is a possibility. I recently had a student write a manifesto. She didn't know what a manifesto was, but another student suggested she write one after she described in her prepitch group what she wanted to accomplish—a rant about social issues from the viewpoint of a babe-in-the-woods persona named Alice. She studied several famous manifestos, including the *Declaration of Independence* and the Unabomber's manifesto (*Washington Post* 1995) plus Wendell Berry's poem (1985) "Manifesto: The Mad Farmer Liberation Front." And then wrote her own.

During the two-day prepitch phase, students do not need to know a firm answer to any of these questions, but they need to wrestle with them. Often they ferret out a more concrete writing idea as it becomes a writing project, or they abandon their idea for a different one as they answer these questions. This weighing, abandoning, clarifying exercise is the critical aim of all creative and productive struggles.

After students grapple with the five essential questions, they spend the second prepitch day sketching out and practicing their pitch. Some students want and need to write their pitch out. It's not required. Some memorize it; some decide to shoot from the hip. They can practice pitching with their groups during class, and on the third day, we're ready for pitching proper.

PITCH

During pitch days, everyone sits in a circle on the floor. I feel this is important because it makes the whole crew present and engaged—no desks divide us, no chairs in which to slouch. It's also reminiscent of the Fire Pit and not as intimidating as standing up in presentation mode. I draw a name out of a hat, and that student gives her pitch. In a two-minute pitch, students answer all five questions:

1. What was the genesis or spark of your idea?

2. What genre/form will your project take?

3. What is a brief summary—including the purpose—of your project?

4. What are your manuscript goals for the project?

5. What are your 4P goals? (publication, performance, presentation, or production)

While students are pitching, I keep time and make notes for assessment. When I meet with them during our postpitch conference, I refer back to the pitch notes, discussing the pros and cons of their ability to conceptually capture their idea for the class and also to delve further into their next-step plans for this project.

The rubric I use is student designed and has six categories aligned with the elements of the pitch, so students are evaluated on whether or not they have communicated the genesis of the project, their genre/form, and a summary/purpose of the project with enough details that the project is clear to the class. Students must also express specific and measurable manuscript goals, including word count or number of pieces, such as blog posts or poems, for the final product. They must also state a specific place where they want to reveal their final product to the real world, either by performance, presentation, production, or publication. Finally, they need to communicate all of these things in a two- to five-minute time frame.

You can always modify what you ask students to include in a pitch, of course. The point is for them to articulate their plans for the writing they want to do. After all, this "elevator pitch" skill is one that will serve them for a lifetime and extends far beyond writing projects. And as always, if you have less time for the pitching process, consider having students pitch to small groups (who haven't already heard their ideas) instead of the whole class.

So let's look at the specific elements of the pitch more closely.

What was the genesis or spark of your idea?

In a normal elevator pitch, the pitcher would start with a hook—a question, startling fact, or scenario—because he would want to pique the interest of the intended audience. However, we start our pitches at the most natural place: the moment of inspiration, the genesis of the writing idea. Students explain the circumstances that gave rise to their writing project. For some it will be a character they have discovered or the memory of something that was reignited by a writing prompt; for some it will be the recent events of their lives, or something in the news, or even an assignment from another class that has them jazzed.

Sarah found the genesis of her project in a boy she met at a summer camp who had challenged her. She pitched:

> I need to write about this guy named Ryan and his relationship to happiness, bravery, and me. This project comes from two things: (1) my need to write about those five weeks of my life, and (2) my interest in spoken word poetry. The first is self-explanatory—there are stories there that I need to tell. The second is from, I started binge-watching YouTube poetry this summer too.

John found the genesis of his project in his passion for all things sports. He pitched:

> For this project, I would like to write blog posts about college football. College football is going on, and I thought, you know, there's only so many chances for me to take on this project. I'm excited to try this out and I have an interest in sports journalism.

What genre/form will your project take?

Hopefully by the time students give their pitch, they've determined what form would be best for delivering their idea, even though the form may evolve, as we witnessed with Victoria's original guide that morphed into a personal essay. When Sarah was inspired to write about a person who challenged her, she gravitated toward spoken word poetry because spoken word could support the emotional and literary range she needed to address, confront, rage, question, and demand things of her subject, whereas John chose the blog because he wanted to write short, analytical pieces on college football, and the form of a blog post supported all those criteria.

When I taught writing traditionally, I often started with form, and then students would have to stick their idea into a preselected (by me) form that had not been chosen by them. By providing them a preselected purpose with a predesigned form that may or may not fit the personal exigence that gave their idea its power in the first place, I was sabotaging the most essential element of their personal writing growth. Their ideas might be pinched because the shoe they're winching their ideas into didn't belong to them.

When a writer initially comes upon a writing idea, the form may not necessarily be the first thing that presents itself. Figuring out what the writer thinks about the idea is most important. I can't emphasize this often missing step enough. In other words, the student needs to wrestle with her own purposes to identify her form.

In the pitch, however, students state the genre or form they're going to pursue for their writing idea because they have decided (after much work in the prepitch days) that this form is the best fit for their purpose. Specifically, they state what purpose they have for the project (to argue, to narrate, to inform/explain, to express) and what form the writing will take: blog, essay, short story, poem, and so on.

Everything about project-based writing is used in the service of student inquiry and the discovery of purpose. If a student doesn't know what a vignette is, give her a copy of *The House on Mango Street* (Cisneros 1984) and ask her what she notices about the way each piece is written. Turn her on to *Vine Leaves Literary Journal*, an online literary journal (http://www.vineleavesliteraryjournal.com/) dedicated to vignettes.

Does she know how to write a screenplay? Maybe not. But the best way to figure that out is to actually write a screenplay! So, shoot her a couple of YouTube channels dedicated to the craft, like *The Script Lab* (https://www.youtube.com/user/thescriptlab) or *Lessons from the Screenplay* (https://www.youtube.com/channel/UCErSSa3CaP_GJxmFpdjG9Jw). Give her a couple of chapters of David Trottier's *The Screenwriter's Bible* (2014) or Blake Snyder's *Save the Cat* (2005) or Syd Field's (2005) *Screenplay*.

I'm not saying she will become an accomplished screenwriter after viewing a few videos and reading some craft books, but she will learn the material more deeply and use it more intentionally because her learning is connected to her driving need to tell her story. And the writing that will come from this screenwriting foray will be a learning experience itself, a lesson that will apply to all other forms of thinking and writing as well.

What's a brief summary—including the purpose—of your project?

The summary is a conceptual snapshot of the final product, and at this stage of the game, the picture may not be crystal clear. It doesn't have to be an exhaustive, extensive plot treatment, but it should show evidence the writer has moved beyond the idea stage to convince the class that this writing project has taken shape in his mind.

Sometimes the summary poses the questions a student will answer in the course of writing. Here's part of a pitch from Avery who wanted to write a couple of blog posts that delved into why Donald Trump was such a popular candidate:

> He ran for president before, with nearly the same ideas and opinions. When he ran then, he gathered only a miniscule amount of votes and dropped out soon into the race. But he had nearly the same ideas and opinions. Why now has he become so popular? Because fate just ended up on his side? Did God himself cast a blessing onto Donald Trump to allow him to suddenly be so popular?

This student doesn't need to know the answers to these questions at the time of the pitch. That's what the writing will uncover. When a student pitches a short story, she doesn't need to know how it will end, but she needs to be able to summarize the big ideas: a pregnant environmental scientist has to decide between her family and her career; five men driving home from a Halloween party accidentally kill a small child and decide not to report it; a family of Syrian refugees experience hospitality when they come to Kentucky. (All of these are actual ideas from my class.) The summary portion of the pitch only "sells" us on the viability of the project and provides the class with evidence that the writer has built the necessary springboard to jump into the writing.

What are your manuscript goals for your project?

Word counts are an essential parameter for real writers because they are important to the magazines, publishing houses, websites, and other media outlets where writing is published. Word counts and guideline boundaries are also important for all kinds of writing connected to careers. Conceptualizing word count or chapters or page count in relation to a writing project is an important skill to develop for the college and career ready student.

In the pitch, students declare their manuscript goals, a specific measurable amount of writing that can be tracked daily, such as word count, page count, chapter count, or the number of blog posts or poems a writer plans to produce.

Allowing students an opportunity to impose their own word count limits for the final product is empowering and instructive. It allows them to make a specific, measurable goal as one does for weight loss or personal bests in running. Word counts create a target for their daily actions as a writer.

I still assign word count expectations for the proposal and reflection so that students have an expected range in which they can propose and reflect. Most teachers impose word counts as an assessment tool because students write too little instead of too much and the product is thin and underdeveloped. But an underdeveloped argument is not the fault of too few words; it's the fault of an underdeveloped idea.

Like form, the purpose and genre of the proposed project often dictates the word count or number of pages. Before the project cycle, I explain in very, very generalized terms that the word counts for various genres are largely determined by the publishing market and the author's intentions for the piece. For example, microfictions and vignettes are small, 100 to 1,000 words, and short stories range from 1,500 to 30,000 words, and novels can range from 50,000 to 150,000 words. Blog posts are usually about 500 to 750 words, whereas a *New Yorker* essay weighs in at 10,000 words. I also explicitly instruct students that their publication goals may largely determine their manuscript goals. If they know the Scholastic Art and Writing Awards contest for a critical essay has a word count range of 500 to 3,000 words, they will want to tailor their manuscript goals to hit that mark.

I don't want students focused on the word count during the flow of creation—I want them only to write, write, write. But during the framing of the project, it's helpful to think about the space on the page for their work.

> Whether you decide on length requirements or your students decide on their own, be sure to determine length by the word count, not the number of pages. In the world of writing outside school, word counts rule the day. Students need experience working with word count guidelines just as they learn to craft a Twitter message in 140 characters. "How much space do I have to do the work I want to do with this writing?" is one of the most critical questions a writer asks.

What are your 4P goals?

The last element of the pitch is for writers to declare how and where they will reveal their work to an audience outside the classroom. 4P is my shorthand for performance, presentation, production, or publication, all ways in which students could choose to move their work from the comfy confines of our writing community to a larger arena.

At some point in their writing process, the awareness of a specific real-world audience raises the stakes for their writing quality. The facts must be checked and correct. The grammar, usage, and organization need to help, not hurt, the final project if for no other reason than to "not look like a fool," according to Joe.

Let's say a student writes an informative/explanatory piece about raising organic garlic. He could read his piece on his YouTube channel (a production) or read it as a part of the local Farmer's Market open mic (performance) or create a digital story around it and present it to the local Future Farmers of America club (presentation) or submit it to a magazine like *The Progressive Farmer* (publication). The power of 4P is the weight and accountability that a thinking public audience will be reading or watching this piece of writing.

POSTPITCH

After the pitch, the class questions the pitcher more specifically about the project during a five-minute Q and A. Students can ask any question they want to ask of the pitcher, with the understanding that the pitcher may not know the answer to the question, and he doesn't need to know it. The questions alert a writer to what a curious, interested audience might want to know about a project.

Here's an example. Karlee wanted to write a children's book about a bird, a reindeer, and a little girl. The reindeer can't talk about his emotions, and his inability to express himself was making him sick. The little bird and the girl help him get in touch with his feelings, so he doesn't have to bottle everything up. The pitch was great, and Karlee knew how she wanted to execute the relationship between the three characters.

"I like this idea. What's the time frame?" Rayny asked.

"What do you mean?" Karlee asked.

"Does the story take place in a day or a week or what?"

"Oh, I think it's maybe going to be, like, one season, maybe spring, but I don't really know," Karlee said.

"Why is it a reindeer and not just like a dog or a cat?" Gwen asked.

Karlee shrugged. "I don't know. I just like reindeers."

And the conversation continued that way until there were no more questions or five minutes were up, whichever came first. I time these vigilantly.

I don't have any rules for the Q and A, but I do tell the class to let curiosity be their guide. Students just ask questions that occur to them naturally during the pitch. I tell them: "If a friend of yours sat down with you in the cafeteria and said, 'Hey, I want to write this children's book, and once I'm finished it, I'm going to read it at our church to help some really shy kids,' you'd be curious and interested, and you might say, 'That's cool. What's it about?' or 'Who are the characters?' or 'Tell me the plot.' Those questions might be the very thing that helps the writer begin her piece."

After the Q and A, I ask one person in the room to summarize what we're voting on. This summation from another person other than the pitcher is helpful in that (1) it guarantees no one has checked out mentally, and (2) it also refocuses the class after the back-and-forth of the five-minute Q and A. I will choose this person at random, and she sums up the pitch in a single sentence: "Jared wants to write a 300-word letter to the editor of the *Herald Leader* to complain about the way Lexington treats the homeless population in Phoenix Park. Let's vote."

Then the class votes on whether the student's idea should proceed to the proposal. It's a very simple thumbs up, thumbs down. If you convince more people to thumb up than thumb down, your project gets the green light.

The voting is a very important part of this process because it's real world. A burgeoning filmmaker needs to interest a production company, an inventor needs to interest prospective investors, a journalist needs to pitch his feature idea to get the assignment. Voting makes all students accountable to their community in a real way.

It's not a war tribunal, but it does create the kind of communal pressure on the writer to bring her best pitch to the table. Some students are anxious during the first pitch, but mostly because the process is new to them. As long as they've thought through their idea (and they've had several opportunities to do

> The value of students knowing what other students are writing about is significant on so many levels. Even if you decide not to do the whole pitching process, it's worth it to have students share what they are writing about with other students (if they've chosen their own topics). You can do this very simply in a round-robin where students just say a sentence or two about their topic.

this in class) and they can articulate their thoughts (I encourage them to practice their pitch over and over), they will be successful.

Last year, out of 180 pitches, only eight projects were voted down. Not once was a project voted down on the basis of idea or subject. In all eight instances, the student either had not prepared the pitch well or the project was too much or too little for the project cycle. In other words, ideas are never rejected, but the viability of a project is. When students are asked to repitch, they are forced to evaluate the scope and range of their idea or their own ability to articulate its feasibility, just like a real-world project would necessitate.

Here's an example of one of the eight voted-down projects. The student wanted to write a couple of novel chapters about something dystopian, but nothing else about the project was clear. There was no character awareness, no plot, no narrative ideas. When pressed during Q and A, he was only able to offer that the plot was going to be "awesome and full of philosophy." After several questions from the class, it was apparent he had not thought about any of the details of the project. The class voted down his pitch, so the next day he repitched to spend a project cycle working on a storyboard with a plot outline, character sketches, and a 1,000-word novel treatment. The second pitch was approved by 100 percent of the class.

One of the beautiful things that happens as a result of the pitch process is that everyone in the room knows and anticipates what everyone else in the room is writing about. When one of my students decided to write about the cultural phenomenon of "princess balls," other students, as they researched for their own projects, would send her links for her project library when they ran across something they thought she could use.

Student's identities then become defined by the projects they tackle: Ruby becomes known for her work on agricultural topics, David becomes known as someone who writes about film and culture, Taleah is known for embracing projects about issues of race and feminism. This communal research creates a network of awareness and participation that creates an even stronger sense of community and shared action.

HOW DO STUDENTS WRITE A PROPOSAL?

After all students have completed the pitch, each student writes a formal 300- to 500-word proposal during class the Monday after pitch week. The proposal is similar to an executive summary or an abstract of a project, and all the elements of the pitch are present in the proposal: the genesis, the genre/purpose/form, a summary, plus manuscript and 4P goals. The audience is me, the teacher, and the proposal is explanatory/informational in purpose. I ask students to clarify their final ideas about their writing projects that they have gleaned from the prepitch, the pitch, and the postpitch Q and A. The student has thought about her idea a great deal by the time she sits down to type up a 300- to 500-word proposal, so her aims are more concrete and more refined.

Here's Ruby's 316-word project proposal for writing a series of blog posts about raising chickens:

> For Project #1, I have decided to take my readers on an adventure into my chicken coop. This spring, I made a questionable impulse buy of eight baby chicks, and I have spent the last six months figuring out how to care for them. By the fifth month, I'd decided I had figured the chicken thing out, and somehow convinced my mother to drive three hours to pick up two miniature ducklings. With ten birds in my small backyard, I suppose I could consider myself a real urban poultry farmer—or a rooster for that matter (at least to my hens). Needless to say, I have discovered a whole new world—a world worth blogging about. I have decided to blog about my experiences and discoveries to share with the poultry-keeping community and poultry lovers alike. Over the next six weeks, I am going to publish four new blog posts, as well as about four old, reedited blog posts from last year, onto my new website on WordPress. com. For my four new blog posts, I am going to write about laying hens,

keeping chickens in the summer, raising ducklings, and an about me page. I am also going to revisit my previously written blogs about feeding, leg bands, and raising chicks. My goal for these pieces is to inform and entertain people who either already have or are considering getting chickens or ducks. I hope to provide enough information to hold the interest of an audience that is already informed about poultry without boring them, as well as those who are widely uninformed about poultry without confusing them. Each blog will be approximately 500–800 words. I plan on incorporating pictures and videos on my page as well so every time you enter my site, it is like you're walking into my backyard. Overall, expect to see a new website and at least seven blog posts!

Even though the pitch and proposal are activities connected to the world of business, neither is designed to teach kids how to pitch or propose an idea, although those speaking and writing benefits are corollary. The activities support and engage students as they handle, whittle, and shape an unformulated idea. Each time they think and write about an idea that started as a small flicker in the pit of their stomach, they illuminate its shape and clarify its form.

6

Planning the Work:
Product Goals and Project Scheduling

After discovering an idea, then pitching and proposing the writing project, students will next spend some time planning the work. In the project-based writing world, that includes scheduling the tasks and setting goals. Setting product goals is a great starting place for young writers because it allows them yet another opportunity to think through the writing idea and see the end product as clearly as possible. The task of goal setting illuminates the final product, not the process, in the mind of the writer. As she works through the messiness of drafting, with equal parts success and failure, she will be able to return to these goals to target and reassess, or perhaps abandon these goals for the sake of better, more clarified goals as the final product emerges. Product-specific goals also serve as a basis for inquiry and testing as the student begins the daunting task of creating actual text out of the wisp of an idea.

Backward design is a term I explicitly teach my students, using the Common Core as an example of a product that was developed from the question, "What skills and proficiencies should a graduate of the United States education system possess?" Once that question was answered, a set of standards was created, designed in a backward fashion from the answer, leading a student through developmentally appropriate, progressively aligned skills and proficiencies to create a creative, globally competitive, twenty-first-century, critical thinking graduate. I also tell them teachers use backward design a lot to develop curriculum. We start with the goals of our unit and work backward to determine what skills—delivered through sequential lessons—need to be mastered to achieve the goals.

When I introduce my students to the concept of backward design, I want them to start thinking about their end product, the final thing they ultimately reveal to the world, in terms of discrete elements that support the goals they have for the piece. The goals should be squarely grounded in the purpose of the piece and should be crafted with the end product in mind.

They ask questions like:

- What is my vision for the end product?

- What is important to me about this piece of writing?

- What is my purpose?

- What do I want readers to know when they're finished reading it?

- What do I want readers to feel when they're finished reading it?

- What do I want readers to do when they're finished reading it?

- What elements of writing—logical sequencing, developed characters, clear organization, effective claims, compelling evidence, graphic imagery, sharp scenes—will impact my readers and reveal my purpose?

HOW DO STUDENTS CREATE PRODUCT-SPECIFIC GOALS?

Prior to students building their product goals for the first time, I fishbowl with a single student, so the class sees the process by which I question, clarify, lead, and inquire to generate goals that are valuable and clear to the writer. They will be doing this exercise with a partner or with their writing group.

"Taleah, do you mind being on stage for a minute?" I say.

"Not at all, not at all," she replies, her high heels clacking on the chair legs as she stands up and makes her way to the center of the room where I have arranged two chairs facing each other.

Taleah has already pitched, so the whole class knows what she is doing— a collection of poems that explores her African American ancestry and culture. She's written her proposal too—eight poems that follow the journey of a young girl as she discovers the history of her family. The class voted 100 percent in favor of this project, so now she's wrestling with goal setting.

"When you think about this poetry collection, what goals do you have for the final product?" I say to her.

"I want people who read it to remember this and get angry," she says.

"You want it to have an emotional impact?"

"Yeah."

"Good. So when you read a poem and it has an emotional impact on you, what causes that?" I say.

"The way it makes me feel," she says.

"Right, but how does a poet make a reader feel something?" I ask.

"The details, the images?" she says.

"Perfect. So maybe one of your goals might be imagery? Or details?"

"Yeah, I like imagery as a goal."

Taleah ultimately chose imagery, purpose, mood, and structure for her four goals.

What I hope to illustrate with Taleah's example is the power and necessity of helping students tease out four goals that will guide them as they write the first of many drafts. The goals will change as the product emerges because writing is an evolving, recursive practice. Students need to know that writing is not a one-and-done activity. We set goals, do some writing; we set more goals, do some more writing.

Once Taleah decided on the four targeted elements of her product, I wanted her to think about how these elements contribute to her initial conception of the final product and to her ultimate purpose, which was, "I want people to remember this and get angry." Does she want her imagery to be startling, graphic, sensory, or subtle? Does she want her structure to be narrative, lyrical, associative? What is her purpose? If she recognizes how these distinctive elements of writing contribute to audience impact, she can manipulate the imagery, purpose, structure, and mood to garner that.

WHY DOES GOAL SETTING MATTER?

The purpose of creating a goal statement is not merely to learn how to create goal statements, just as giving a pitch and writing a proposal are not to learn how to give pitches and write proposals, although both are laudable and transferrable skills.

The purpose of all these framing and planning activities is twofold. I want students to have multiple opportunities to think and write and discuss their own writing before they begin to write the actual product. I also want a student to feel proprietary toward her own work and to recognize the importance of her artistic

> Goal setting is important because it forces writers to think about what they want to achieve with their writing before they start. The process I describe here can be modified in several ways. You might have students set just one or two goals for a piece of writing, instead of four. The language of the goals might be more or less sophisticated to match your students' experiences. The format for writing the goal can be more or less structured. And goals might be set for their own process rather than (or in addition to) the narrative, rhetorical, or poetic quality of the final product. The point is for students to use their goals to start writing a piece with specific intentions in mind.

choices. All of the activities in the project-based framework are designed to create self-possession in students while simultaneously generating a lot of writing and reading in the service of an idea they have chosen to pursue. Setting goals for a product is an important part of establishing personal agency over the work.

So if you are worried that the goals aren't "right" or that there are more important goals to pursue in an argumentative essay than the ones your students come up with, calm yourself with the knowledge that the goal itself is not the most important part, but that *making* the goal is the thing that gives students independence and writerly confidence. Making goals for your own writing says, "I am the god of this product. I am the creator," and it illustrates a powerful connection for students when they realize that what they do on the page, with words and sentences and paragraphs, ultimately determines a reader's experience.

What literary component brings about an emotional or logical satisfaction in the reader? Isn't that, after all, what our purpose is in writing? To make the reader feel things, to act, to wonder, to be entertained, to be informed?

My goal as a writing teacher is to help Taleah understand how all of these discrete elements of her craft are used in the service of communication. I want her to begin her own inquiry, such as, what is my responsibility as the writer, as the encoder of words that a reader will eventually decode? How does my diction, for example, influence my tone, which in turn influences my audience?

HOW DO STUDENTS WRITE GOAL STATEMENTS?

Once students come up with four goals they'd like to pursue, I explicitly teach a lesson on how to write a product goal statement.

The goal statement should have three distinct parts:

1. one writing element a student thinks is important for the success of his piece (imagery, purpose, organization, and so on)

2. a goal for that element in relation to the larger work (in other words, the "job" of that element in service of the whole piece of writing)

3. an "in order to" statement that connects the element and the goal, showing how the element will lead to the goal.

Here's an example of a goal statement:

> *The imagery in my poetry* [the element under consideration] *should be clear and detailed* [the specific goal of that element] *in order to evoke emotion* [the purpose of the element in this particular piece of writing].

I use this formula to help struggling writers identify and define their goals, not as an absolute prescription by which writing success or even goal-setting success will be achieved. For students who may not have written goal statements for their writing before, this formula helps them think through the connection between writing elements and their goals for the finished product.

Here's an example of four goals another student, Jenna, wrote. She had proposed a story about a teenager who has a monster living under her bed. (In Chapter 8, we'll return to these goal statements to see how Jenna crafted her inquiry questions for her inquiry draft based on these original statements.)

Goal 1: The pacing in my short story should be smooth in order to keep the reader's attention and move the story forward.

Goal 2: The voice in my short story should be unique in order to make a connection between the reader and the story.

Goal 3: The world building in my short story should be clear and play along with the events in the story in order to create a realistic and developed plot.

Goal 4: The syntax within my short story should be coherent and understandable in order to create a readable and good-sounding piece.

Notice that pacing, syntax, and voice are all in the service of keeping the reader's attention. She's clearly interested in a connection with the reader to create a readable piece of fiction. The only goal outside that scope is world building, which Jenna indicates serves to create a realistic and developed plot.

WHAT IF MY STUDENTS DON'T KNOW EXPOSITORY OR LITERARY TERMS?

Still you might be saying, "What if my students don't even know what tone is?" Let's pause for a minute and discuss *tone* as an example for an extended meditation on this issue of direct instruction of literary terms and genres.

Not only does developing product goals help clarify the final product for the student, the act of goal-setting serves as embedded formative data for the teacher. During the goal setting process, it will become clear when students don't understand the difference between tone and style. These clarifying data give birth to a differentiated minilesson on tone. You can then deliver a lesson on how tone differs from mood, which differs from style, with learner buy-in because his pressing need demanded this lesson.

Just as decades of research on grammar instruction has shown that isolated grammar activities do not improve a student's ability to apply grammar rules to improve her own writing, teaching isolated literary terms and devices to students does not improve their ability to manipulate them in the service of their own writing.

Students may have heard these terms for their whole English language arts career—*tone, audience, voice, purpose, idea development, style*—and they may be able to rattle off a definition—yeah, yeah *diction* is word choice, and *syntax* is sentence structure—but until they have to use these terms as a writer, even the smartest of your students won't truly know what those terms mean.

We often teach tone as a literary device that needs to be excised, dissected, and analyzed in a piece of literature (external), but the best way to teach tone is to have students identify it in their own writing (internal). When writing must be built rather than analyzed, the writer's focus moves from the external to the internal, from the knowledge to the application, and creative problem solving becomes real.

The key in writing instruction is to teach students to understand how diction and syntax support their organically emerging tone and cut away anything in revision that would create tonal whiplash. And the first step on that road of awareness is the struggle of defining *tone* for themselves with the teacher as their intrepid guide.

Then tone isn't some abstract device used by old spinster poets, but a vibrant, essential element that is naturally discovered through the course of writing. Students attempting to impose a tone on a piece of writing (because my teacher's rubric says I have to have a tone!) will have a clunky, artificial piece of writing; students who allow tone to emerge as a by-product of their fully realized attitude toward their subject will have a tone that naturally supports the overall effectiveness of the piece.

A PLACE FOR STUDENTS TO START

Goals are neither right nor wrong; they just are. Students can start anywhere, and as they grow in their awareness of themselves as writers, they become more sophisticated and specific as goal setters. As such, the goals may be broad or strange, but you can hear and see students wrestling with their work as an animated product and the concept of themselves as managers of this yet-to-be-born living thing.

For example, Michael wrote, "The writing is vivid so that a film picture is playing in the reader's mind." Nathan projected this goal: "The main character should be characterized so that he seems unreliable, mysterious, and flawed." And Avery wrote, "The world established is well defined, but above all fun." Do you hear how unteacher, unstandard, unrubric-y those goals are? Do you hear how each student's goals are specific to her current conception of the product she is about to produce? There is anticipation and hope in those goals, and a little bit of fear, but she has staked out her own vision, for what it's worth.

You will always have students who have no idea where to start with goals for their final product, so I provide them a broad sampling of criteria to consider based on the purpose they have chosen as seen in Figure 6.1. These elements are taken directly from the College and Career Readiness Standards for writing with some additional input from me on the narrative and poetry columns.

FIGURE 6.1

Some Criteria Used to Set Goals for Different Modes of Writing

PROSE			POETRY
Argument (nonfiction)	**Informational/ Explanatory (nonfiction)**	**Narrative (fiction or nonfiction)**	
Claims, including introducing and establishing precise claims and counterclaims	Topic, concept, or idea, including introduction, development, and establishing its significance	Conflict, including introducing and establishing tension, protagonist, antagonist, and the stakes	Purpose, including introducing and establishing narrative, lyric, or dramatic
Evidence, including developing relevant, logical, and credible evidence	Details, including significant and interesting details that are concrete and specific	Context, including point of view, narrative distance, setting, time/place	Imagery, including vividness, clarity, and sensory details
Organization, including cohesion, unity, and logically sequenced claims and counterclaims, with credible evidence	Organization, including logically sequenced sections and transitions, between major sections of the text to create cohesion	Organization, including scenes that follow naturally and sequentially, building or in contrast with one another for effect	Structure, including poetry form or lack of form, line breaks, line lengths, stanzas, verses, rhyme, meter
Language, including diction and syntax, that supports the argument's claim	Language, including diction and syntax, that supports the development of the topic, concept, or idea	Language, including diction and syntax, that supports and reveals characterization, narrator voice, and overall narrative effect	Language, including diction and figurative and poetic devices, that supports the poem's overall effect

continued

PROSE			POETRY
Argument (nonfiction)	Informational/ Explanatory (nonfiction)	Narrative (fiction or nonfiction)	
Style and tone, including appropriate tone and formal or informal style depending on the audience	Style and tone, including appropriate tone and formal or informal style depending on the audience	Style and tone, including appropriate tone and formal or informal style depending on the characters, narrator, and overall narrative effect	Style and tone, including tone appropriate to the subject, audience, and persona, and style that is consistent and appropriate for subject, audience, and persona
Mechanics, including standard English grammar, usage, spelling, capitalization, documentation, and formatting for selected purpose and form	Mechanics, including standard English grammar, usage, spelling, capitalization, documentation, and formatting for selected purpose and form	Mechanics, if appropriate for the selected purpose and form, including standard English grammar, usage, spelling, capitalization, and formatting	Mechanics, if appropriate for the selected purpose and form, including standard English grammar, usage, spelling, capitalization, and formatting

Students create and share their four goals in their Google Drive project folders. I then use their goal statements during my conferences as a starting point for conversations. Like a ruler for measurement, students refer back to these product-specific statements, sometimes tweaking them or abandoning them in favor of a more clarified goal as their writing product emerges. They might choose another goal or another compositional element as the final product transforms and grows during the cycle.

HOW DO STUDENTS CREATE A PROJECT SCHEDULE?

Project scheduling helps students define their project in terms of time and the central reality of their own process. Organizing time is a very personal issue. Some of us are good at it; most of us are bad at it. Students don't have a lot of practice at it because they've never been in control of their time for most of their academic career.

At the beginning of each chapter in Randy Bomer's *Time for Meaning* (1995), he includes a short meditation on time. I recently shared this quote with my students as it relates to managing our projects:

> *To live in time successfully, we have to learn to manage our own deliberate being in time. That is, we have to learn to embody in time our best intentions, to do what we mean to be doing, to live on purpose. If we want to support our students as they craft their literate lives, we have to give up the authority to micromanage their work and instead return the authority to them. (41)*

For my class, I create a project template calendar in Google Drive and type in all the school events that might interrupt our class time: school pictures, bus drills, pep rallies, and so on. I also write in all the firm due dates for activities, such as the pitch, proposal, inquiry week, community score. Students then make a copy in their Google Drive of the template and create their own project calendar, scheduling specific work for days we have individual studio time.

Students use the calendar for two purposes: to set daily task goals at the outset of the project (in one color text) and to post their daily efforts during the project cycle (in another color text). With a quick glance at their project calendar, I can assess how their targeted goals match up to their actual daily work.

Project scheduling is important for two reasons: it allows students to develop the necessary skill of breaking down a large project into small manageable parts, and it allows students to feel in control of and accountable for their time. Be prepared for students to completely bomb at scheduling the first couple of projects. For many, a giant expanse of unstructured time yawning out before them is, frankly, scary. By project three or four, they have figured out their own work habits and their writing pace, but they need to be supported mightily because they often fail at time management early on.

In her personal reflection after her first project cycle, MacKenzie writes:

> *When I turned in my project calendar, I honestly didn't know if I made any sense because I didn't know if I could do all the things I said I was going*

to do. I'm used to doing writing assignments on the night before it's due. While writing this piece, some days were slow and others I would be writing and the bell would ring, and I thought we'd only been in class ten minutes.

Project scheduling creates an awareness of how little or how much students can manage their own time, which is one of the first steps to becoming intellectually and academically independent. And even though failing at this is part of the learning process, managing time and increasing productivity are behaviors that can be learned.

Figure 6.2 is a sample of what a blank calendar for one project cycle would look like during the second six weeks at our school.

During the blank calendar days, students have the entire ninety-minute period to pursue their individual projects. I call this highly valued commodity "individual studio time," which we will discuss in Chapter 7. For now, just understand that the key to creating a workable project calendar is guiding students in thoughtful consideration of how much or how little time each phase of their project will take.

Katrin proposed a screenplay which followed a young female character named Daya Vargas as she explored her identity in relation to gang life. Katrin wrote in her proposal, "I think the juxtaposition often found between religious practices/superstitions of gang members and the violence and crime they commit is interesting." Katrin had already completed one project cycle and produced the first fifteen pages of this screenplay. For this project, Katrin was adding fifteen more pages that would "follow Daya as she attempts to assimilate to mundane high school life and her inability to fully do so, slipping back into gang activity over and over again, eventually starting a high school gang war." Figure 6.3 is an example of Katrin's schedule that includes both my imposed project deadlines (in italics), her projected goals (in bold), and her actual daily work (plain text).

Notice how real-world this calendar is. This is project management with all the hitches, glitches, and diversions of a real-world work environment. This calendar represents a student who is learning how to manage her time in relation to the demands of the outside world and her vision for the product.

FIGURE 6.2

Project Cycle Calendar Template

MONDAY	TUESDAY	WEDNESDAY	THURSDAY	FRIDAY
September 19 A *Pre-Pitch*	September 20 B *Pre-Pitch*	September 21 A *Pitch Day*	September 22 B *Pitch Day*	September 23 A *Pitch Day*
September 26 B *Proposals due*	September 27 A *Product Goals* *Project Calendar* *due*	September 28 B	September 29 A	September 30 B
October 3 A	October 4 B	October 5 A	October 6 & October 7 *FALL BREAK*	
October 10 B	October 11 A	October 12 B	October 13 A	October 14 B *Inquiry drafts* *Due*
October 17 A *Inquiry Week*	October 18 B *Inquiry Week*	October 19 A *Inquiry Week*	October 20 B *Inquiry Week*	October 21 A *Inquiry Week*
October 24 B	October 25 A	October 26 B	October 27 A	October 28 A *Final Drafts,* *Reflections & IEF* *due*
October 31 A	November 1 B	November 2 A *Community* *Score*		

FIGURE 6.3

Katrin's Project Two Calendar

MONDAY September 19 A *Pre-Pitch*	
TUESDAY September 20 B *Pre-Pitch*	
WEDNESDAY September 21 A *Pitch Day*	
THURSDAY September 22 B *Pitch Day*	
FRIDAY September 23 A *Pitch Day*	
MONDAY September 26 B *Proposals due*	**Research on Mexican gangs, types of gang activity, and the 8-sequence structure of a screenplay.** I didn't exactly stick to my note of note editing until I had a whole list compiled of what I need to target, but it's alright. Today, I finished compiling said list and then mainly focused on differentiating the dialogue between Daya and Zanita more in the scene where Daya cleans Zanita's cut.
TUESDAY September 27 A *Product Goals* *Project Calendar due*	**If you want to, begin dabbling in the first scene of the screenplay on Celtx.** Finished goals and calendar. Worked on Celtx. Screenplay is so difficult to get back into! Learning curve's what's up.
WEDNESDAY September 28 B	**Spend a total of 30 minutes or less doing research on Mexican gangs. Plot out scenes leading up to the inciting incident.** Focused on giving Antonio more screen time to lengthen the plot up to the inciting incident and to build a better relationship between him and the audience. Got a good amount of work done today in comparison to the usual.

continued

THURSDAY September 29 A	Spend a total of 30 minutes or less doing research on Mexican gangs. Plot out scenes leading up to the inciting incident.
	I probably spent about 50% of the class time doing research. Instead of plotting like I should've done, I wanted to go ahead and start writing because I felt the need to, but I had no clue where to start and I stared at the computer screen a lot. I think I need to get a better grip of the world I'm trying to build. I need a plan. As for writing, I began writing backwards from the inciting incident. Not much progress on that. Tomorrow, I think I'm not even going to get my laptop out. I'm just going to sit down and plot and make a solid decision because I'll keep on wasting time if I don't.
FRIDAY September 30 B	Spend a total of 30–45 minutes or less reading "The Kids Are Alright" and/or doing research. Keep plotting out scenes up to the inciting incident.
	Almost 100% research today, which, even though it wasn't planned, I felt really needed to be done. A good mix of plotting was in there too, and it looks to me that the inciting incident's going to happen way before page 15 in this screenplay, so I think I can afford a day more of plotting if need be (in studio, that is). Solidified something about my [screenplay] writing today- plotting is a necessary friend. My screenplay skills are incredibly rusty at this point (I need to review technical formatting and the like over the weekend), but I feel better about the work I got done today.
MONDAY October 3 A	Finish reading "The Kids Are Alright," return, check out another screenplay if not already done over the weekend. Write 2-3 pages.
	Read two pages of the screenplay. Oops. I'll pick back up on that during lunch, probably. I did, however, write today! Even if it was just a little over one page, I feel like I wrote something that's pushing the screenplay forward. It's not just disorganized write-whatever-comes-to-mind writing. Plotting is truly magic. Scene one- check (or almost check?).
TUESDAY October 4 B	Read half of screenplay you checked out. Finish at home. Write 2-3 pages. Ideally, write a scene.
	Finished reading "The Kids Are Alright." May or may not have gone through the emotions in class. Took notice of the subtleties of Nic and Jules' deteriorating relationship and what Jules does to compensate. I wish the ending with Paul wasn't as abrupt, but I guess he is a pretty horrible person for doing what he did after infiltrating their lives.
	Finished writing scene 1. Started the second. God, I need to stop using reading and research as an excuse not to write. Will be taking those off my calendar and doing them at home instead
WEDNESDAY October 5 A	Get yourself another screenplay (or two, for time's sake). Write 2-3 pages. Ideally, write a scene.
	Forgive me, but my god. I don't know why I did this to myself. I knew I wasn't great at screenplay but screenplay is incredibly flooring. Wrote almost a scene. Feels like nothing, though.

THURSDAY October 6 FALL BREAK	**Finish reading screenplay. Make sure you've written closer to 12 pages at this point.** Definitely did not read the screenplay. Didn't even look at it. However, as I'm not close to meeting my 12 page quota, but in terms of pacing and the timeline of the screenplay up to the inciting incident, I think I'm at a good place.
FRIDAY October 7 FALL BREAK	**Make sure you've written closer to 12 pages at this point.** My screenplay is simply moving faster than I initially anticipated!
MONDAY October 10 B	**Write 2-3 pages. Ideally, write a scene.** Maybe wrote 1-1.5 pages. Not exactly my goal, but I wasn't expecting much anyways for today. The plot is moving forward, I got stuck on a scene so I moved on. Maria Salvadora has been introduced. Daya is finally headed towards her BFF's house (no name yet). Building that relationship from there, and I plan to let Daya's inner violent gangster come through in the scenes to come. I foresee an issue in keeping it short, but I'll just have to push through and write. Overall, quite happy with my work today!
TUESDAY October 11 A	**Write 2-3 pages. Ideally, write a scene.** Wrote a little over two pages today. I'm getting started on a bunch of scenes, but I'm not really finishing them right away. I know this is unconventional for most, but it's actually helping me because once I have a clearer idea of where each scene is leading to up to the inciting incident, I'll be able to fill in the spaces in between. I wrote partial scenes up to Antonio finding out what his last-chance job is and Daya pulling Nita away from a fight (leading up to Daya showing her inner gangster). I'm afraid I'm moving too slow. Still pretty happy with the amount of writing I got done today!
WEDNESDAY October 12 B	**Write 2-3 pages. Ideally, write a scene.** Guess who totally forgot PSAT Registration was today? This lady. Suddenly feeling robbed of writing time. UPDATE: Despite the claims from earlier, still did not write a home. Pat on the back, friend!
THURSDAY October 13 A	**Write 2-3 pages. Be at or finishing the inciting incident scene.** Started scenes all the way up to the scene before the true inciting incident scene. While I did not actually finish any scenes, I feel good because I know the direction the screenplay is headed up until the inciting incident! Now, all I'll have to do for tomorrow is fill in the blanks in between. However, I still feel like I'm not as in touch with any of my characters as I want to be, especially Daya. I need to sit down and make an executive authorial decision about who Daya is as a person. I've gone back and forth on this since before I proposed this project, and I'm afraid my different "versions" of her are getting mixed up into the screenplay. For statistical purposes, I wrote about 2 pages today.

continued

FRIDAY October 14 B *Inquiry drafts due*	**Revise and finish up like a crazy person!** Stop freaking out, and don't wait until 11:50 pm. Well, I definitely had more work cut out for me than I anticipated. I wrote for several hours (maybe six? I don't know, it was a lot) today and still, however, came up a page shorter than my my shortest proposed page count manuscript goals. The time writing versus time thinking timer at the bottom of Celtx is such a cruel form of mockery, too! Either way, I turned in my screenplay about half an hour late (which really pisses me off) but I decided I'd rather turn in something late than something incomplete. That was one of the hardest decisions I've made for this class, and I take the whole blame for turning this assignment in late. I could say I was busy and all, but I'm sure everyone else was as well, and it's honestly more about priorities. I think the scenes up to the inciting incident are rushed, but I can always expand on them in revision and after hearing what my peers have to say. Anyways, I feel liberated. Time for sleep.
MONDAY October 17 A *Inquiry Week*	**Read pieces for sayback.**
TUESDAY October 18 B *Inquiry Week*	**Read pieces for sayback.**
WEDNESDAY October 19 A *Inquiry Week*	**PSAT!**
THURSDAY October 20 B *Inquiry Week*	**Read pieces for sayback.**
FRIDAY October 21 A *Inquiry Week*	**Read pieces for sayback.**
MONDAY October 24 B	**Sift through annotations and comments. Do not get distracted. Once, and only once, you've finished compiling a lists of points to hit on for revision, start revising!** Change of plans. Workshop day today. Did not revise at home.
TUESDAY October 25 A	**Revise. Don't cry.** Revised. Didn't cry. But I was a little lost on revising. This always happens the first day– I'm overwhelmed looking at my list of areas/issues to target that I start on one and start another and another before I finish one and so in the end, I'm left with a lot of loose ends to tie up. Time to re-evaluate and get a better revision schedule going.

continued

WEDNESDAY October 26 B	**Revise. This isn't so bad, is it?** For once, I feel I had a decent work day! I zoned in on a particular part of the screenplay (the first two scenes, for some reason; I guess trying to clarify the world I was building). While it's not finished yet, I spent significantly less time staring at the screen and significantly more time improving and laying the virtual tracks down. Feels good to be productive. Maybe I should try it more often!
THURSDAY October 27 A	**Final Revision** Didn't feel like I got much work done today. I don't know- I'm stuck on how I want to develop the relationships between characters and how I'm going to give Antonio more screen time. I also may have to revise the way Antonio dies and the specifics of his job. Thus, I'm worried that I'll forget to change the little details in between. Gotta focus in on one issue tomorrow.
FRIDAY October 28 A *Final Drafts, Reflection & IEF due before midnight Saturday 10/29*	**REVISE** Conference with Ms. Prather today. Got great, holistic takeaways and areas to target, so that makes the revision process easier! I'm pretty satisfied with the work I accomplished today. I'm mostly just adding more dialogue (dialogue that matters and doesn't just fill up space, of course) to the scenes I already have and trying to tie up loose ends from yesterday. I mostly looked at Antonio in the airport and trying to deepen his struggle with swallowing the pills (this definitely still needs to be developed after today) and deepening/clarifying the relationship between Maria and Antonio (added a bit about thow Maria wants Daya for the business, but Antonio will never let her). I'm also adding to the scene where Antonio and Daya walk down the sidewalk. I added a tissue paper flower for the Day of the Dead, and this flower will resurface soon. Good thing I get off work at 6:30 tomorrow, because I get the feeling I'll be working on this until midnight Saturday to tie up loose ends!
MONDAY October 31 A *Community Score*	
TUESDAY November 1B *Community Score*	
WEDNESDAY November 2A *Community Score*	

If you're not in full project-based writing mode, then students may be working on their writing at home, for a finite part of each class period, for one full day a week, or in myriad other configurations of time. But no matter what, there is a period of time between when the writing starts and when it is due to be finished. By asking students to plan a schedule for how they will get the writing done, with the time they have in mind, you'll be doing wonders to help them develop one of the most critical skills of project management for writing or anything else. Just remember, students will be more and less successful at staying on schedule, just as adults are, but the process of thinking about scheduling is still vital.

One thing I reveal up front to my students is there's no real way to know how long each step of the process takes, but there's value in setting goals. It takes me about five hours to write a 750-word blog post, but it takes me twenty hours to write a 1,000-word feature magazine article because I need to interview people and research facts. It took Thomas Jefferson seventeen days to write the Declaration of Independence; William Faulkner wrote his masterpiece *As I Lay Dying* in six weeks; Ralph Ellison wrote for forty years on *Juneteenth*, his massive 2,000-page second novel that was whittled down to under 400 pages when published posthumously.

Teaching students how to tolerate and manage the unknown is the beauty of project-based learning, and that includes anticipating the tricks of that wily saboteur: time. Project scheduling asks students to recognize the real-world skill of working toward deadlines, both self-imposed and ones set by their teacher, their college professor, their boss, or their clients while recognizing their own proclivities for sabotage and distraction. Managing deadlines well is an essential component to becoming a healthy, functioning adult.

What I think is fascinating about Katrin's calendar is her self-awareness. The project schedule becomes a mirror she holds up to her learning to make adjustments as she examines the positive or negative results. Her project calendar is less a tool for project management than a work of art itself.

As you can see, there is no right or wrong way to schedule a creative project. Think about that. There is no correct method for a writer to schedule his time. What matters is that he does schedule his time based on his goals as he understands them at the time of scheduling. The needs of the project, the needs of the student, and the needs of the process dictate how time is divided and appropriated. The only way you can fail at project scheduling is to not schedule, which is exactly how many long-term writing projects are managed. They are delayed and avoided until the last minute when people start tearing out hair and gouging eyeballs. Even with a project schedule, students still succumb to hard-to-break habits, like watching YouTube videos or whispering to friends, but at least they are forced to become aware of their own tendencies when they record them.

Whatever students actually do during class (including wasting time, procrastinating, zoning out) goes onto the daily tracker. Because the Google document has been shared with me, both the student and I can see where her goals are over or under her actual performance, which can result in some great (and not so great) conference conversations. Perhaps her goals were too lofty, perhaps the project was too thin, perhaps her daily efforts were protracted and laborious. The project schedule shows it all. It's neither right nor wrong. It's just data a student can use to learn about her habits.

HOW DOES PLANNING LEAD TO SELF-DISCOVERY?

The planning process can be very difficult for some kids because it requires two simultaneous, yet opposite cognitive approaches: the student must be able to conceive his original idea, which is unwritten, intangible, and shapeless, while also proclaiming tangible goals, aiming for targets, and designing a schedule that delivers this yet-unwritten thing by a very real deadline.

When I conference with students, we look at their project calendars and figure out lessons we can learn when it's time to schedule other projects. One student may be lightning fast at writing but a sluggish researcher, and another student collects information easily but has trouble organizing, framing, and structuring his argument. These powerful data are not only differentiated but can be used by both the teacher and the student for learning. It's self-discovery at its best.

This is how real writers work every day—managing deadlines and courting the muse at the same time. By tapping into both hemispheres of their brains, student writers must learn to balance the right brain's need to dream and weave and hoot and howl with the left brain as it establishes goals, sets aims, and declares timelines that will deliver. The student must occupy both realms: as a writer taking risks and as a project manager becoming disciplined.

For the writer, all possibilities that can be used in the execution of his work must be on the table; for the project manager, only the delivery of a quality product by the deadline exists. The writer says, everything is possible. The project manager says, let's narrow this show down a bit, OK?

7

Doing the Work:
Individual Studio Time, Project Conference, and Project Library

The pitches have been given, the proposals submitted, the goals set, and the project calendars are looming in their Google Drives. Enough hand-wringing and ramping up: let's write!

WHAT IS INDIVIDUAL STUDIO TIME?

Individual studio time is the label I use to describe any extended writing time where my students stare down the blank page and attempt to wrestle the subconscious into the conscious. In my class, the lights go down, students roll away in their nooks and crannies, and we write and research and read and write some more. Individual studio time is a great opportunity for students to learn about themselves as writers and thinkers, but it's valuable for the teacher also, who is able to work one-on-one with students in a quiet, productive environment.

As with any project-based learning approach, students need lots and lots of time to discover, to research, to create and re-create. Individual studio time *is* instructional time, but it looks and feels very different. The clamor of instructional demands—bell ringers, exit slips, minilessons, major lessons—look busy, like the business of education, but these must be quieted regularly and frequently to create silent and sustained time for just writing.

Sometimes we teachers interrupt those silent times in the form of instructional busy work. Yes, journaling, short freewrites, and open-response writing contribute to their repertoire of skills, but asking students to engage in extended writing time will increase writing fluency and build the cognitive and linguistic muscle memory of going deep into subject matter. Sustained work time is essential.

Individual studio time can and should be scheduled all throughout the project cycle, for the generation of ideas, the actual writing of the piece, and the reframing after the piece has reached a certain shape. How this block of writing time can be carved into your schedule will be up to you and your students. Your day-to-day schedule is unique to your classroom demands, but the key is to protect and devote large blocks of time to self-directed writing. Students are learning by doing, and they need time to do this.

Setting the tone for productive individual studio time is crucial. Here are a few ways to increase productivity while allowing students to learn to manage themselves during studio time.

SET GROUP NORMS

After students understand the framework of project-based writing, I ask them to draw up a set of classroom norms for managing individual studio time. I ask students what they need from me, each other, and from themselves. Your students will come up with a great list, I promise you. Some of the norms that have surfaced from my classes have included:

- Put forth your best effort always.
- Respect the community with support and silence—the Golden Rule.
- Productivity is goal #1.
- No loud music allowed.
- Silence is a must.
- Hold each other accountable.
- We are all leaders.
- Be mature human beings.
- Don't bug people during studio time.
- Keep on keeping on.
- Set daily minigoals to stay motivated.

Allowing students to set norms for studio time feels less like a teacher-dominated school environment and more like a community of like-minded artists who are sharing a space. The norms are printed out and posted in the classroom as a reminder that our classroom community enjoys student-established and student-determined personal freedoms, but those personal freedoms do not obstruct or violate the rights of the larger community. These norms are golden if problems surface in the community, either individually or collectively.

SETTLE INTO WRITING

During a regular day, students move through the high school cattle chute at breakneck speed. When they screech into your English class, they need a moment to settle into a zone that is meditative, creative, and solitary.

For years, I was a bell-to-bell advocate, and I still feel strongly about engaging students immediately, but now I employ a soft start to each class that signals the shift from the hustle-bustle hall to the serene, creative space necessary for writing.

As soon as the tardy bell rings, I project my online stopwatch on the whiteboard to signal "countdown to zero," which means students have three minutes to take care of any business in the room. This business might be getting a laptop out and turned on, finding the right pillow, or getting a cup of coffee. I also use this time to make any announcements, take attendance, give those students who I'll be conferencing with the heads-up, or just open the floor for anyone who wants to say something for the good of the group. As the stopwatch ticks down, I ask students to settle in, to shift their focus from the external, social huzzah to the internal, individual hmm.

At the beginning of the year, I'm very intentional about initiating mindfulness and presence toward our writing. However, as the year meanders on, most students don't need me to remind them to settle in as they begin to observe and practice their own self-selected routines of settling. Here are a few transitional strategies I employ.

> You may have more or less time for students to work on writing in class, but whatever time you do have for this, remember that it is very difficult for writers to *just start*. This is especially true when the writing comes from the student's own thinking and is not in response to any prompt. As much as possible, give students a little time to transition into a state of mind that's ready for writing.

Engage with Meditation

I am both a fan and a practitioner of mindfulness and meditation for stress reduction, concentration, and relaxation. Last year, one of our physical education teachers, who has taught a class on controlling stress for years at Lafayette High School, charged the whole staff with becoming more mindful and meditative. Her P.E. students created several three- to five-minute videos of breathing and meditation exercises designed to relax the body and quiet the mind.

Sometimes I will play one of these videos as a means to tap into the calmness necessary for concentration. Sometimes we just observe a few moments of silence and breathing. Sometimes I lead students in a quick body scan, starting with the head and ending with the feet, releasing stress and mobilizing their inner resources for creativity. I encourage them to develop their own means of initiating the concentration necessary for writing.

> How much you can do to create different kinds of work spaces in your classroom depends a lot on class size and square footage. But it's important to remember that physical space matters to most writers. Some write best at desks, but others prefer a less confining space. A writer working with lots of notes and artifacts might need a table where she can spread things out. You might invite students to help you reimagine possibilities for how space is used in your classroom. Ask them, "What could we do to this space that would best support you and your writing?"

Engage with Personal Rituals

During my twenties, my writing ritual included smoking a few cigarettes and belting down black coffee. However, in my forties, my ritual has changed to lighting a candle, making a cup of tea, and donning my favorite heavy sweater and wool socks. All writers have rituals that signal to their brain it's about to get all writerly up in here. For some, it's getting a special pen or doing a particular writing exercise. For others, it's listening to a song, reading a poem, or looking at photography or art. I encourage my students to develop rituals of their own, both in my classroom and in their own private writing time.

Part of ritual building has to do with the comfort and safety of the physical space. I have both traditional and nontraditional seating—couches, futons, and beanbags—and I encourage students to find the space, including on the floor, where they will be the most comfortable and productive. Unless they encroach on others' solitude and creative space, they can sit anywhere. Electing one's own space is part of ritual building and sitting in a special place can often prepare the mind to work.

Disengage from Technology

Each teacher needs to make his own decision about how he will deal with digital distraction. I love cell phones and use them for many instructional purposes. Tweeting, pinning, insta'ing, and snapping poetry are great ways to quickly publish. I tweet out writing prompts and share craft articles on social media for my students.

However, just because digital devices are a boon for one instructional posture does not mean they are beneficial across the board. For sustained, concentrated effort needed for writing, the fragmentary nature of cell phone use is a complete disaster.

When I write, I put my cell phone in another room so I can't hear my Facebook messenger. I know the lure of social media is even greater for my students. Because every element and area of the brain is necessary for writing, students can cut their productivity down to nil with cell phone preoccupations. So I am adamant about no cell phone use during individual studio time.

Some students want and need music to accompany their writing; music helps them relax into the mind space necessary to create, but I require all tunes to be accessed through an online playlist or cached on a device other than the seductive iPhone.

All of my students have a laptop they can use if they wish during individual studio time, which is great for researching, reading, and writing. But when the world is just a key stroke away, there are infinite enticements for a writer looking to avoid the act of writing. I don't save students from this lesson by initially correcting them unless they are bothering someone else or there are other behavioral considerations. Allowing kids to waste time and then record it in their project calendar is a powerful instrument of self-awareness.

Of course, if time wasting is habitual, I step in and inquire, while being curious and empathic.

Prime the Writing Pump

One of the hardest things to do as a writer is to just pick up a pencil and start moving it across the page. Sometimes asking students to write at the beginning of studio time on a topic other than their writing project gets them in the frame of mind, and fires up the neural pathways that will help them settle into their projects. Sometimes, at the beginning of the year, I set the mood for writing with writing. I'm very judicious about this because some kids want to jump right into their own projects, and they see this forced writing prompt as an encroachment on their time. But others need it.

A common mantra I use in my class is, "Take what you can use and leave the rest." If they need to write at the beginning of class, I have a writing prompt on the board or a poem to read, and they can use it. I might lead anyone who wants to join in a poetry transcription or a written reflection from a question I pose. I do this less and less as the year progresses, but writing at the beginning of class is the thing some students need to get ready to write.

INCREASE PRODUCTIVITY

Once students have found their comfortable spot, settled into the rhythm of writing, they may have no problem zoning out the rest of the world and staying on task, especially because the project is one of personal selection and interest. However, even professional writers skid to a halt when they come to a tough spot in the writing—a problem of phrasing or a puzzle of structure. This is the moment when a student can choose to give up, resign to defeat, or dig in and figure out the problem. I encourage students to do a couple of things to develop the skill of digging in.

Silence the Critics

Just like real writers, students carry around in their heads the voices of the naysayers who say they can't think, can't write, can't succeed. Some of those voices will be teacher voices. Some will be the voices of the arbiters of morality or writing quality. Some will be the voices of parents, peers, or self. Whatever the identity of those who chatter in our brain, it's a helpful exercise to shut them up before we start writing. I use two exercises for this.

In *Bird by Bird* (1994), Anne Lamott suggests that a bit of visualization is necessary for silencing the critics that threaten to stifle your writing before you even begin. I share her advice with my students:

> Close your eyes and get quiet for a minute, until the chatter starts up. Then isolate one of the voices and imagine that person speaking as a mouse. Pick it up by the tail and drop it into a mason jar. Then isolate another voice, pick it up by the tail, drop it in the jar. And so on . . . Then put the lid on. (27)

In *Writing Alone and With Others* (2003), Pat Schneider's trick is also built on visualization. She says to imagine yourself standing in a desert, and far off in the distance, a bus rattles toward you in a cloud of dust. The bus screeches up beside you and stops, opens the door, and out tumbles every critic who's ever leveled a nasty opinion on your work—second-grade teacher, your priest, your grandmother—and they all come yapping off, and you let them yap, but ultimately, they get back on the bus, and the bus trundles off. Then in the distance, you see a second bus. This bus pulls up even with you, and the doors open and out steps every champion of your work—your mom, your best friend, your third-grade teacher—and they tell you your voice matters, that you are enough. But eventually they get back on the bus too, and soon you are alone in the desert, and it is time to write (22).

Make a List

Some students need to carve up the class period into tinier, more clarified goals each and every day. These goals meet the immediate needs of the three questions I encourage students to ask themselves at the beginning of each work day: Where am I now in my project? Where am I going in my project? How can I get there?

One sophomore, David, gave this advice about managing individual studio time to incoming ninth-grade students who would be taking my class the next year: "Just assess yourself at the very beginning of the day and say to yourself, 'What do I need to get done in the next hour and a half?'"

Learning to set minigoals is a really important project management skill that, like so many others, extends far beyond writing. Whenever students have a stretch of time in front of them where they are choosing how to get their work done, consider teaching them how to set minigoals for the work they will do. The format can be as simple as an old-fashioned to-do list, which brings with it the enormous satisfaction of checking off the goals as they accomplish them. When students return to their work at a later time, the minigoals are a record of where they have been and can help them imagine where to go next.

This clarifying exercise focuses the work for a small period of time or for a few singular processes, like outlining or revising. Sometimes students don't know how to make minigoals, and I step in, encouraging them to tackle the most difficult task first, whatever that might be for them. In time management circles, this metaphor for doing the hard stuff first is called "eating the frog," the idea being if you get up every day and eat a live frog, your day can only improve from there. If you have a writing task you've been avoiding, do that first thing and get it out of the way, so you can look forward to another more enjoyable task.

Take a Break

Classic writers from C. S. Lewis to Thoreau extolled the benefits of long strolls in the woods as the key to creative problem-solving. Your students can't go wandering in the woods for long stretches at a time, but they can take short breaks and do something else to give their brains a chance to recalibrate.

I encourage students to set a timer, using an online stopwatch, for a five-minute break. Having a definite period of time to relax, ponder, get a cup of coffee or a drink of water, stretch their legs increases productivity rather than decreases it. In fact, just a few minutes of daydreaming, staring out the window or watching a bug crawl across the floor, allows the mind to actually focus more on the project at hand. During the daydream, the mind free-associates, which is why we often have those eureka moments when we are doing mundane tasks like the dishes or laundry. During the breaks our mind makes the necessary connections, in a relaxed and unfocused state, which reveals the answer to whatever problem has stymied us.

Shift Cognitive Focus

Shifting cognitive focus is similar to taking a break, but the aim is focused on the writing project from a different angle. All projects require some measure of the following activities: reading for content, reading for craft, reading for models, researching for content, researching for craft, researching for models, and writing, which could be writing as a draft or writing as researching and reflecting.

If a student has met a dead-end in writing, suggest he shift to researching or reading. If both of those prove to be distractions, set a timer for twenty or thirty minutes of reading or researching, then dive back into the writing. Having a secondary activity for a creative process that is connected to and in support of the project is important for both brain breaks and productivity.

HOW DO STUDENTS SET UP A PROJECT LIBRARY?

In Stephen King's (2000) *On Writing*, he says, "If you want to be a writer, you must do two things above all others: read a lot and write a lot" (86). In addition to all the peer texts that students read (in a single project cycle, students read over 100 pages of their peers' prose and poetry to prepare for Inquiry Week), students are also reading for three main purposes during individual studio time: reading for research and content, reading in their chosen genre for mentor texts, and reading about the writing craft. As students find texts that support their projects, they each create and maintain a document called the project library, where they document texts read during their projects.

Outside of primary classrooms where teachers use them to track fluency and sight word banks, reading logs feel burdensome and contrived to me. However, because many of my students are not avid readers, I needed an instrument that encouraged using texts to inform the writing while giving students freedom and independence in choice. This is not a reading assignment; it's a way to cultivate reading practice, a lifelong dependence on self-motivated research, and interaction with written texts of all kinds. I don't want reading to be something a student has to do, but something she wants to do, the selection driven by her need to know and her passion for her present project.

Do real writers do this? Yes! As a freelance writer, I keep a running source list for every story I complete, which includes magazines, blog posts, book chapters, excerpts, and any bibliographic information along with quotes, summaries, and paraphrases for all the material I read to inform myself on the subject about which I'm writing.

Reading in any curriculum is only meaningful if students see it in service of their lives, not as an isolated, contrived activity meant to fulfill a state mandate. Reading in a project-based writing classroom serves the purposes of inspiration, information, and mentoring in a way teacher-assigned reading cannot.

The important component of reading in a project-based writing class is students select what they read based on the needs of their project. The reading informs students about their chosen subjects and inspires them to see the possibilities in the genres they have chosen. The reading is tied to and supportive of students' projects, which creates immediacy and relevancy to all student reading choices.

> If you want to direct your students' reading more intentionally, you could divide the class into three reading groups—those who are writing arguments, those who are writing narratives, and those who are writing informational texts—and select texts to support each form of writing. Each group would work as an independent literature circle and respond to the craft text in relation to the project they are currently pursuing. Two days of individual studio time could be dedicated to these profitable discussions.

EXAMPLES OF STUDENT PROJECT LIBRARIES

While researching for her chicken blog, Ruby's reading strategy was threefold: she read technical articles about how to blog; she read a lot of blogs she found interesting in order to be inspired by the possibilities of what was out there; and then she also read a great deal about chicken farming, not only to learn about the subject for her own blog, but to know what hadn't been covered, what small niche in chicken raising she could fill. Figure 7.1 is a sample of Ruby's project library where she recorded three kinds of texts she was reading while writing her chicken blog.

FIGURE 7.1

Ruby's Project One Project Library

	Title	Summary	Response
Writing Models	Fresh Eggs Daily www.fresheggsdaily.com	This blog is written by a woman in Maine who raises vegetables and chickens. The blog uses lots of pictures throughout of herself and her chickens.	I like the layout of this blog, and I like how she uses pictures and text.
	Chickens 101 www.chickens101.com	This blog is all about raising chickens in your backyard.	This blog doesn't have a lot of fancy stuff—mostly text, not pictures. Not as visually appealing, but lots of good information.
Content Research	Backyard Poultry magazine http://countrysidenetwork.com/magazines/backyard-poultry-magazine/	This magazine has feature stories about particular poultry issues and featured farmers plus how-to articles and just funny articles about coops and chicks. Part of a larger network of magazines called Countryside.	This is the first magazine I got after we purchased our chickens. Its like *People* magazine for chickens.
	BackYardChickens www.backyardchickens.com	This website is managed by Rob Ludlow, who co-wrote *Raising Chickens for Dummies*. It has hundreds of articles on here about chicken coop designs, chicken breeding, raising, and chicken culture.	I loved this blog! The message board is a great place to get quick information. This blog has been around for fifteen years and shows what can be.

continued

	Title	Summary	Response
Craft Articles	How to Start a Blog www.artofblog.com/ how-to-start-a-blog	This is from *The Art of the Blog* website, which has a lot of how-to posts on setting up a blog with a complete guide from WordPress.	This was my go-to guide for all questions blog related.
	Top 20 Agriculture Blogs www.seametrics. com/blog/top-agriculture-blogs	This is a list of the top twenty agriculture blogs on the web. Some of them are connected to larger corporations or magazines, but a lot of them are just regular people, scientists, farmers, or bloggers with agriculture interests.	I noticed that there is a huge difference in layout and eye appeal to each of these. Some of them were hard to read.

Ruby chose and recorded all three types of reading in her project library, a simple table that helps students track the scope of reading texts they read during each project. They record the title of the article, Web post, blog, or wherever they find their reading, along with a short summary and a personal response that reminds them of why they read the piece in the first place or jogs their memory about what they are using from that particular article.

John pitched and proposed a novel set during World War II about two brothers who are drafted to fight. John's project library ranged from research reading to genre reading. Following is his list of readings for this project:

- *The Things They Carried*, historical fiction novel by Tim O'Brien concerning his time in the Vietnam War.

- *A Prayer for Owen Meany*, fiction novel by John Irving with subplot of Vietnam War and events of the 1950s through 1970s.

- "The Draft and WWII," article discussing the draft that took place during World War II and providing images of draft notices (The National WWII Museum).

- "Your Number's Up!," article by Carl Zebrowski (2007) explaining the process of the draft that took place during World War II.

- "Were They Always Called World War I and World War II?," (Nix 2013) article discussing how these wars were actually referred to during the respective times that they took place in.

- "Occupations & Jobs in the Late 1930s to Early 1940s: A Picture Narrative," article by Dianne Heath (2011) discussing jobs of the time period that this project takes place in and providing images.

John selected the texts as he needed them for research to write the first chapter of the novel where the brothers are drafted. As we conferenced, I suggested that John also read two chapters from James Scott Bell's *Write Great Fiction*: *Plot and Structure* (2004) book, specifically the two chapters that deal with plotting and scenecraft.

HELPING STUDENTS SELECT TEXTS

When I introduce the concept of a project library to students, I tell them, "Anytime you bookmark or save a link online, that article should go in your project library." The concept of bookmarking virtual texts is synonymous with the real-world gathering and gleaning that goes on when writers research for content or genre.

Students don't have to read whole texts for that text to go into their project library because that's how real writers work. I don't read whole gardening or recipe books if I want information about how to fight aphids on my roses or how to make a killer butterscotch pie; I often hunt and peck through the table of contents for the chapters pertinent to my interest or need at the time.

In the appendix, I've compiled a list of great texts in our classroom library that are genre-specific for students to use. I often recommend specific chapters from these texts, per the issue (dialogue, narrative pacing, developing ethos, integrating quotes, and so on) they may be dealing with in their project. I also keep an old-school vertical filing cabinet in my classroom with drawers for nonfiction, fiction, poetry/drama, and argument, containing folders of articles, mentor texts, chapters from these books.

My classroom library also has old copies of the slicks, *The New Yorker*, *Oxford American*, *Vanity Fair*, *Esquire*, and *Harpers*, all harboring great examples of in-depth essay, articles on true crime, short fiction, movie and food reviews, and character profiles from sports figures to country singers. I also keep on hand old copies of *Poets and Writers*, *Writer's Digest*, and the *Writer's Chronicle* (you have to be a member of the Association of Writers and Writing Programs to get the chronicle, but if you make friends with a nearby university English department, they almost always have old copies to hand down to an eager high school English teacher).

HOW DO YOU CONFERENCE WITH STUDENTS ABOUT PROJECTS?

Throughout the project cycle, I conference with students, both formally and informally, using their four product goals as my inquiry guide. I shuttle current research to them about their topics, provide craft resources for their project libraries, offer encouragement, and answer questions, but largely I want students to be as independent as they can be while shaping their writing projects.

If I see students who are becoming frustrated to the point of giving up or acting out, I step in and help them get back on track. But taking a hands-off approach during the creation stage allows students to build their own instinct that they can figure out language, organization, and logic on their own. This productive struggle is incredibly powerful.

Once the creation process is exhausted—I define that as once students have taken the piece as far as they can take it or run out of vision for the piece— it's time to get some feedback. Students who have less vision and autonomy than others will be the first to arrive at this point, and many of them need feedback to take the next step, but they may not be ready to give the piece to the class. In every class, I have about five students who are in this category, and I may shepherd their pieces a little more directly, conferencing with them until they have a complete piece to submit to the class for inquiry and feedback.

In a six-week project cycle, I conference with each student three times— once at the beginning of the cycle to discuss the student's pitch, proposal, project schedule, and product goals, then mid-cycle in a small-group conference to check in on the progress of the project, and then after the cycle to conduct a post-project interview using a rubric to guide our discussion (Figure 11.6). There are dozens of resources out there on conferencing with students about writing, so I will only add a few things to the already existing conversation.

MAJOR ON MANAGEMENT, MINOR ON WRITING

During the initial conference, I push students to think about their own learning in relation to the project framework, not because the framework is the most important thing, but because the framework is a tool they can use to manage many writing projects, not just this one.

Writing is a skill that is its own best teacher. Students learn to write by writing, and I want to keep my hands off that process as they work independently toward the final product. So I conference mostly with students on their time and task management, checking their project calendars to make sure they haven't scheduled themselves too thin or too thick with tasks, checking their product goals to make sure they align with purpose, form, and genre, checking in on their project libraries to make sure the texts they are reading are appropriate and supportive of the project. I will step in if I see students are becoming frustrated or off-track, but I want them to problem solve.

The framework is there to assist in the management of the project, but the product itself is a creation of the student's. In each conference, I want to bring their awareness to how they are managing that writing as much as the writing itself. As I meet with students, I ask, "Have you made your word count goal? Have you logged your daily tasks into the project calendar? What texts have you chosen for your project library? Are you referencing your goals as you start shaping your inquiry draft? Have your goals changed? If so, how and why?"

ASK AUTHENTIC QUESTIONS

The key to conferencing is to allow the student to talk more than you do, and to guide them toward discoveries instead of micromanaging or being overly critical. Yesterday an infographic from the research of Kylene Beers and Robert Probst popped up in my Twitter feed. The table compared two kinds of teacher talk: talk that checks for understanding and talk that creates understanding. The differences are glaringly apparent to students. As Beers and Probst (2016) explain, students reported that when teachers asked students questions to check understanding, the questions came off as inauthentic. The students recognized the teachers already knew the answer and were just checking to see if the students knew what the teacher wanted them to know. Conversely, when teachers asked questions to create an understanding, students identified these questions as more authentic because the teacher did not know the answer (57–58).

When I approach the project-based writing conference, I have to remind myself I don't have the answers. Sometimes I don't even know the questions as they relate to the individual student project. In this mutually discovered inquiry, teachers and students meet over a shared goal—to understand themselves as writers and to grope along together as the student creates something that's never existed before.

Yes, teachers most likely understand argumentation, narration, and informational texts better than their students because they've presumably had more practice at writing, and they've had more opportunities to fail and learn. But it's imperative that students fail and learn also, with a teacher there to inquire and to lead students into inquiry themselves as they gain a greater understanding of their unique process.

At the beginning stages of writing, my writing-oriented questions are completely low stakes. "Hey, what's up?" is one of them. Questions like the title of Carl Anderson's book on conferencing (2000), "How's it going?," are also a perennial favorite. Other questions, such as, "What's working today?" or "What's not working today?" or "Tell me where you are in the process" open the door of inquiry for the student and allow her some space and time to talk about her concerns without feeling as though she'll be evaluated for doing so.

CONSIDER THE POWER DISPARITY

Because of the delicate balance of power between teachers and students, the ratio of positive-to-negative feedback should be about 5:1 because I want them to be encouraged and continue on. At this stage of their writing process, many students assume that every question you ask is really a suggestion in disguise. This may be because they still aren't sure of themselves as writers and they're looking for direction. Or when a teacher asks a student a question, it's not to truly get their feedback, as Beers and Probst discovered, but merely to suggest and guide students toward a specific answer.

I recently had a conference with Marin who was writing a short dramatic script where this question-to-suggestion ratio seemed to show up.

"Why does the protagonist not appear until the second scene?" I asked, truly interested by this artistic choice. It was a sophisticated, risky move she'd made narratively and it served this particular story, a mystery, very well.

"OK, I'll change it," she said. She immediately assumed I was suggesting she change it.

"No, I don't want you to change it," I said. "I'm interested in how you're building this scene. Why did you make the choice to withhold the protagonist?"

"I don't know. I just did."

"That's good. That's how you figure out the story in the first draft, you start asking yourself these questions: Does it make a better story if the main character does this or does that?"

"Remember when we watched *Casablanca* last year?" she said suddenly.

"Yes?"

"The audience doesn't see Rick until, like, fifteen minutes in."

"Is that what you're aiming for?" I asked.

"I think so," she said.

Although a community is dependent on one another for many things, you want your students to become increasingly independent of you and the community as they grow as writers. They need to start fashioning their own inquiry of their own process and style and arguments.

RESIST THE URGE TO TAKE OVER

Many writing teachers encourage student writers to check in and get feedback at every stage of the writing process, and many students benefit from that. But also be judicious about assisting students during the thinking, writing, struggling part of the writing. Remind yourself that this is their writing, not yours. If it fails, but they've successfully escorted a writing project from idea to publication, there's glory and laurels in learning how to escort, even if the writing project might not be Booker prize material.

Some students want me to read what they've written, and tell them if it's good or not. This desire for feedback is a natural reaction for all writers. They just want to know whether or not what they are writing makes any sense to another human being. And that's OK.

However, continually seeking approval and/or feedback on writing in the early stages from a teacher can stymie a student's ability to develop his own quality regulator. Some students genuinely need help; for others, it's a crutch.

First I ask them if they've read it out loud to themselves a couple of times. If they have, I read what they've written, then return the inquiry to them. "What do you think is good about this?" or "What do you think is kind of clunky in this?"

Remember, the studio time is generative. It's not about proofreading and editing. At this stage of writing, students should only be concerned with getting it down on the page, developing their own ideas, and figuring out how to organize them.

Just as students need to learn to balance their right and left brains, teachers must learn to weigh their own writing knowledge and natural teacher empathy while watching students forge their own processes. Teachers who don't judge wisely regarding this delicate equilibrium run the risk of ignoring a frustrated student or enabling one who might benefit from struggling a bit. Teaching, like everything, is about balance.

ENCOURAGE STUDENTS TO KEEP PLUGGING ALONG

Many conferences I spend just encouraging students to continue with their project and not get discouraged because they've wasted time or haven't been able to find the right voice or can't find the right evidence for an argument they want to make.

Your students will have these moments. One student, Briana, wrote in her final reflection, "Too many times this year I used these ninety minutes of class time to stress about other problems in my life and found myself becoming more and more bored with what I was writing."

When students failed to maintain their individual studio time by the goals they set out in their project schedule, they became aware they were sabotaging their project through avoidance. One student admitted he had spent an entire week researching the right German weapon for a short story set during WWII. He wrote, "Individual studio time, more like Wikipedia time. I valued the opportunity to write, but the ease with which I could goof off was permanently enticing."

Other students obstruct their goals preemptively by bothering others or doing work for other classes. Like the framework of any traditional classroom, these behaviors must be addressed empathically and privately. One of the best classroom management mantras I've adopted in the last five years is one I picked up somewhere online: "Don't be furious; be curious." Students act out when they are confused, frustrated by the process, and a host of other factors. It's my job to find out why.

DELIVER ON-THE-SPOT LESSONS

During individual studio time, I cruise around the room and pop in on students, making myself available if they need a suggestion for a research resource or the answer to a quick craft question. Sometimes several students who are working in similar forms might have a similar question about an element unique to that form, and I might do a small impromptu lesson in one corner of the room.

These lessons are almost always centered in technique—what's the best way to organize evidence in an argument? How do I connect my evidence with my premise? How do I use flashbacks effectively? How can I use indirect characterization to reveal my antagonist?

It would be ideal to have a brief one-on-one with everyone in my class, and with smaller classrooms, you might be able to, but I've found that conferences at this stage often work better when students are grouped by genre.

Right now I have one student working on an article for a nonprofit newsletter, two kids working on blogs, and another student working on a speech for her history class. I could pull these four kids for a conference because they are all working on argumentative texts. If one student has a question about establishing credibility, my on-the-spot lesson on ethos might be something all of them can use, even if they haven't expressed that.

I also have two students working on one-act plays for a Scholastic dramatic script contest and another writer who is working on a TV pilot. If I pull those three students aside for a conference, the on-the-spot lesson might be something on pacing or scene intensity, a technique lesson they all can use.

A FINAL WORD ON DEDICATED WRITING TIME

Learning to sit in a chair and sit in a chair and sit in a chair is the necessary posture of all writers. Learning to stay with the project, to lean into it, to keep going even when the inspiration well is dry is the lesson I want my students to learn during individual studio time. I want them to develop the internal motivation to write instead of relying on the browbeating of some external force (picture me as a Viking coxswain).

However, as much as I want them to develop internal motivation, I must create an environment where individual creation can thrive. Thus, the only and absolute condition of individual studio time is silence. Students may listen to music with headphones, and they may get up and move around the room when necessary, but they are not to talk to each other, only to me in a conference. This is a nonnegotiable. I fiercely endorse and enforce the sanctity of silent studio time because I believe it is only in this time, when all the world and its enticements are shut down, that a student can truly learn about herself and her own mind.

This is where project-based writing and project-based learning part ways. In project-based learning, many of the projects are collaborative in nature and the project necessitates discussion and teamwork, but an individual producing a creative project, such as a piece of writing, needs no distractions or external engagements. We have collaborative moments throughout—prepitch, pitch, say-back sessions, conferences—but during the brute labor of writing, there's only one student and her brain and a piece of paper. It must come to this.

Here's why: writing is thinking, and you need time alone with your own brain to do this precious activity. As my student Colin wrote recently in his writing practice, "Writing is only a small fraction of writing. Most of it is thinking. And all reading is thinking. So literature and storytelling really requires a lot of thought."

Give your students the gift of time and silence to think their thoughts and write them down. It will become their favorite part of the day.

8

Reframing the Work:
Inquiry Draft, Inquiry Questions, Annotations, and Say-Back Sessions

When several writers get together to discuss a piece of writing and give feedback to the author, the exercise is often called a "writing workshop" and the activity itself is called "workshopping" a piece. This activity might also be called a "writing critique" or "critiquing," but the activity remains the same: giving feedback to the writer. The feedback can be valuable or destructive, depending on several variables: the thickness of the writer's skin, the sharpness of the reviewer's tongue, and the trust that exists between the two parties.

In the graduate and undergraduate world, writing workshops tend to follow the pattern of a back alley shakedown. The writer under consideration is bound and gagged, while a small gang of other writers rifle through her short story to determine if there's anything of value there. In Carol Bly's *Beyond the Writers' Workshop* (2001), she likens the process to "low-level, mild, politically sanctioned sadism" (16).

This process has always left me cold because it excluded the person who had conceived and created the thing on the table. I have discovered that a process based on multiple levels of inquiry works best for high school writers. A writer asks questions of himself, of his piece, and of his writing group, and the writing group asks questions, too. Then the writer is able to answer and ask other questions if necessary. In my classroom, we call this process "Inquiry Week. "

INQUIRY WEEK: AN OVERVIEW

In the middle of the project cycle, my students participate in Inquiry Week, a highly anticipated event that students rank as the best part of project-based writing every year when I ask them to rank the elements of the project cycle from most helpful to least helpful. Here are a few of their comments from last year's exit evaluation:

> I have to say that the whole inquiry draft along with the annotations and say-back are my favorite part because it gives me just so much to work with. Also I think it is just timed really well in the process because it comes along when I have questions that I don't know how to answer and getting other writers' feedback on it always really helps with that process." —MICHAEL

> When it rolls around it seems like I am stuck on my piece, need help with how to develop a scene, the characterization is weak, or I just don't see where the piece is going. When this happens, everyone gives me new ideas and says what is and isn't working. This is by far the most helpful thing for my writing that we do in this class. Being able to get helpful feedback on things I need help on and things I didn't know I needed to work on is the thing that helps me get that final draft finished." —MEREDITH

> The inquiry draft and questions are by far the best part of the project cycle. I love Inquiry Week because I like reading my classmates work and having a discussion about the piece. Also, knowing that the entire class is about to read the piece makes me motivated to write something worth reading." —JENNA

The cornerstone of Inquiry Week is self-inquiry, starting when the writer develops four questions (we call these "inquiry questions") that accompany a draft of his work (we call this the "inquiry draft") that will be submitted to the class. Inquiry questions are open-ended questions, such as, "How would you describe the tone of my blog?" or "What would you say my claim is?," that serve as a discussion boundary that prevents the feedback from becoming prescriptive.

During Inquiry Week, several things happen: students post their inquiry drafts with four inquiry questions to our online classroom, and everyone in the class reads each piece. Students have an opportunity to read ahead and annotate each piece or they can do it the night before as long as they come to class prepared to discuss the piece under consideration.

Each student prepares for the discussion by both annotating the draft under consideration and answering the four inquiry questions attached to the inquiry draft. In this way, they are prepared to participate in a process we call "say-back."

Say-back sessions are conducted with the whole group, and during those sessions, the writer gets information from the class about the inquiry questions she's posted with her drafts and has the liberty to ask more questions during her time slot. I will discuss each of these elements in more detail later in this chapter, but for now let me say that we call these sessions "say-backs" because the group's goal is to intentionally describe the work, saying back to the author what they've just read instead of offering suggestions for fixing the piece.

If you have a large class or don't have several days to devote to this part of the process, consider breaking students into small groups to annotate each other's work and participate in a say-back session. You can also reduce the number of questions you ask each writer to bring to the group. When the feedback is shared during the say-back, circulate among the groups to maintain fidelity to the process and take valuable notes on what students need to know about supporting each other as writers.

For a class of twenty-five students with ninety minutes per class over a week, each students gets about fifteen minutes for their say-back session. I create a very intentional schedule, slotting students who have shorter pieces with students have longer pieces so as not to tax the group with lengthy reads each night. Figure 8.1 shows you a sample schedule.

FIGURE 8.1

Project One Inquiry Week Schedule

Friday, 9/2	Tuesday, 9/6	Wednesday, 9/7	Thursday, 9/8	Friday, 9/9
David— 7 pages/ screenplay	Leila— 10 pages/ mixed media short fiction	Briana— 12 pages/ magical realism-fantasy short story	Jenna— 16 pages/ magical realism-fantasy short story	Constance— 14 pages/short fiction
Avery— 21 pages/ screenplay	Katrin— 9 "word" poems	Savannah— 12 pages/ multigenre	Nathan— 10 pages/short fiction	Duncan— 15 pages/ murder mystery
Joe— 10 pages / screenplay	John— 10 pages/novel	Taleah— 10 pages/ memoir	Michael— 8 pages/ novel	Meredith— 6 pages/letters dealing with grief
	Jamin— 7 pages/short story			
Total reading (pages)	36	34	34	35

How Do I Read and Respond?

1. Read the piece through once quickly to get a sense of the whole piece.

2. Read through a second time more slowly to annotate and answer the inquiry questions.

3. Come to class prepared to give feedback to the writer on the specific questions he or she has asked.

4. Make sure all your annotations are completed before 8:00 a.m. the day of the workshop.

How Does a Workshop Work?

1. The writer "runs" the workshop. He or she controls the pace and direction of the feedback.

2. The workshops last about fifteen minutes each. I will keep time.

continued

3. Everyone must speak once before anyone speaks twice.

4. Don't dominate the workshop by providing a laundry list of comments. Give one piece of feedback and then allow others to contribute.

5. You can ask questions of the writer, and the writer can answer or ask questions of his or her own.

6. If you make a comment about something in the text, you must provide evidence from the text to provide context and a reference point for the writer.

7. Listen closely to your peers' comments, so you don't repeat something that has already been stated.

8. If you want to add onto what someone else has stated, respectfully reference their comment. If you want to disagree or qualify what someone else has stated, always respectfully acknowledge and reference their comment in your response.

CREATING GOOD INQUIRY QUESTIONS

The first step toward a robust Inquiry Week is helping kids figure out how to write questions that generate data for their next drafts. Often students won't know how to ask questions that will give them quality feedback. Inquiry questions also need to be written so they provide readers a clear guide for the say-back.

Even though they are the creators of the piece under consideration, some students still harbor feelings of self-doubt about their ability to usher a piece of writing to completion. This kind of student often crafts broad, prescription-producing questions (i.e., Does this suck?) thereby giving their peers an invitation to suggest remedies to reduce suckage. Another kind of student crafts simple yes-or-no questions because she is convinced of her own genius and doesn't plan on listening to the community say-back anyway.

Both types of students are failing to see the purpose of writer's inquiry. Yes, it's to generate feedback, but it's also about developing their own internal writerly scales of judgment, balancing the feedback from the group with their own writer's sensibilities. It's about artistic problem-solving, and it starts with asking the right questions about one's own writing. Here are five ways I help students develop good inquiry questions.

START WITH GOAL STATEMENTS

I first advise students to look at the product-specific goal statements they crafted from the outset of the project. We have used these four initial goal statements during conferences to measure and recalibrate the piece as it has progressed, and these are a great place for students to start fashioning their inquiry questions. Figure 8.2 shows Jenna's goal statements for her short story about a monster living under her bed alongside the inquiry questions she developed to accompany her draft.

Notice Jenna's first three inquiry questions (pacing, voice, and world building) align with the goals she created at the beginning of the project. But with the last goal category, she decides she doesn't care as much about syntax now as she does about characterization. She wants feedback on a broader craft element—how her protagonist has been developed—rather than on the more mechanical element of syntax. Ask students to look at their goal statements first as they shape their inquiry questions to determine if those four elements are still important.

FIGURE 8.2

Goal Statements and Inquiry Questions

Goal Statements	Inquiry Questions
The pacing in my short story should be smooth in order to keep the reader's attention and move the story forward.	How did the pacing help or hurt the story? Are there any parts that are too fast or too slow that cause the reader to be taken out of the story?
The voice in my short story should be unique and aware in order to make a connection between the reader and the story.	How would you describe the voice of the narrator telling the story?
The world building in my short story should be clear and play along with the events in the story in order to create a realistic and developed plot.	In what way was the world that the story takes place in developed and how did that help the reader to accept the events within the story?
The syntax within my short story should be coherent and understandable in order to create a readable and good-sounding piece.	How was Sophie characterized? Was there enough characterization for Sophie being the protagonist?

READ IT OUT LOUD

Another way to determine inquiry questions is to read your work out loud. Reading your work out loud is a way of hearing your own language, how ideas work together, how clauses and phrases connect, how syntax helps or hurts the work. This activity is about listening to your writing as it occupies the air.

I tell students: read your piece out loud two or three times. Each time you stumble over a word or phrase or sentence, mark that place in the text. Once you've done this several times, analyze the vocal bump: a missing word, unparalleled phrases, clunky construction, or lack of clarity, sense, purpose?

Think about the engineer who takes his invention out for that first spin. If he hears a bang or a jangle, he's not going to ignore it; he's going to stop, examine, inspect under the hood a bit. That's the practice I want my writers to develop—don't avoid the bump; embrace it. Figure out why you stumbled when you read it, and get curious.

There are several variations on this age-old revision strategy. A student can ask a friend to read her piece out loud, while the writer, hard copy in hand, follows along and makes notes about what the reading reveals to her, either holistic baubles or small, mechanical errors.

There are also text-to-speech apps in both Microsoft Word and Google documents that will allow the application to read text out loud. The automated reader can read text as fast or as slow as you want and as many times as necessary for a writer to hear the piece. If you decide to experiment with this approach, there are many free text readers available online, such as TTSReader and Acapela Box.

Sometimes I ask a student to read out loud and record it, then listen to the recording, following along with a hard copy in hand. They can record their work with a smart phone voice memo function or use an app, such as Voice Record Pro.

Based on the marked-up reading copy, students can create four inquiry questions for Inquiry Week that are specific and tailored for meeting the needs they've already identified from reading their drafts aloud several times and listening to their texts.

READ LIKE A STRANGER, ANSWER LIKE A WRITER

Another way to develop inquiry questions is to pretend you've never seen this piece of writing before, that a random person on the street just handed this to you and asked you to read it and look for its flaws and its merits. Most writers in the real world are able to do this by writing something, then throwing it in a drawer to marinate for a few months, creating the necessary cognitive break between the creation of a work and the revision of the work. Student writers don't have that luxury.

I tell students: "As you read the piece, what would you ask this writer if you sat down with her over a cup of coffee? In other words, have an internal conversation between yourself as a writer and yourself as a reader."

On a clean sheet of paper or in their writing practice books, students can create a double-entry journal and respond to the text as The Reader in one column with questions about what is on the page, then answer as The Writer in another column about the intentions of the piece, the parts still in their brains. This is a powerful activity for students of all ability levels, and it provides writers with their own feedback before they fashion the questions for inquiry.

Many of the questions that pop up in the read-like-a-stranger activity show up as writer's inquiry questions during Inquiry Week. These are questions perhaps The Reader has posed and The Writer can't answer or would like other readers to weigh in on.

TRIPLE LIST ANALYSIS

Similar to having a conversation with yourself as a reader and writer, this activity asks students to divide a large sheet of paper, oriented landscape, into three columns, wherein they write these three questions:

- What did I want this piece of writing to do?

- What is it doing right now?

- How can I advance this draft to meet my vision?

These are all questions that proficient writers ask as they troll over and over their work. Developing this habit in young writers is critical, and the practice begins with self-inquiry.

Because the piece of writing came from your brain, your brain often supplies the things that are missing. For example, if you offer a precise claim for an argument and you offer compelling evidence to support that claim, you might think that the connection between the claim and evidence is obvious. It's obvious to you, isn't it? But will the connection be obvious to someone whose brain isn't shared by you? Is the connection between the claim and evidence there in the text, but just not developed?

The triple list requires you to honestly assess the work in its formative stage to gain data for the continued project, but it also provides great information for forming inquiry questions for students to use to get feedback during Inquiry Week.

QUESTIONS TO CONSIDER

If a student is still flummoxed about composing inquiry questions, as a last resort, I offer a handout called "What We Talk About When We Talk About," which gives several open-ended questions on arguments, informational/explanatory texts, narratives, and poetry (Figure 8.3).

This resource helps students start the inquiry process, albeit outside of their own creative process. After they use this resource on the first couple of projects, they begin to develop their own specific (and better) inquiry questions.

After students develop four inquiry questions, they type them above the title of their piece, so the questions are the first things a reader sees when the document opens. These inquiry questions frame how the class reads the piece and provide a clear agenda for the say-back session.

Learning to ask questions of an emerging draft is an important skill for any writer. Consider how you might teach students to ask questions of their drafts as the process of writing unfolds. If you're not going to have say-back groups, you can address these questions in individual writing conferences or with written feedback. Even if you and the writer are the only ones who see them, the process of thinking about a draft and generating questions is still valuable. The writer can't help but see the draft differently if he's forced to ask questions about it.

FIGURE 8.3

What We Talk About When We Talk About

What We Talk About When . . .

. . . WE TALK ABOUT ARGUMENTS

What is my main claim? Is it clear? Is it important?

In what way have I established that my claim is important?

How do I establish credibility?

How do I appeal to the mind and heart of the reader?

Do I introduce opposing claims? Are they valid?

How did I organize my claim and counterclaim?

Are they logically connected?

What is my evidence? How do I organize it?

In what way is my evidence relevant?

In what way does my evidence make sense?

In what way is my evidence balanced and unbiased?

How does my evidence support my claim?

In what way do I connect my evidence to my claim?

How do I create cohesion between my evidence and claims?

How does my diction support my argument?

How does my syntax support my argument?

In what way does my tone support my argument?

In what way does my style support my argument?

In what way do I conclude the argument?

continued

. . . WE TALK ABOUT INFORMATIONAL/EXPLANATORY TEXTS

What is my topic? Is it clear? Is it important?

In what way(s) have I introduced my topic?

How have I organized this piece?

How does the formatting that I've chosen help or hurt the organization?

How do the details connect and build on each other?

How do the facts, definitions, quotations, examples, or other information help the reader understand this topic?

How do I transition between details?

How do I transition between paragraphs?

How do I transition between major sections?

What ideas, concepts, or information (related to the topic) do I use in this piece?

How does my diction fit this topic?

How does my syntax help the reader understand this topic?

How does my organization help clarify this topic for my reader?

In what way does my tone help a reader understand this topic?

In what way does my style help a reader understand this topic?

In what way do I conclude this piece?

. . . WE TALK ABOUT NARRATIVE

Describe my protagonist. Describe what she/he/it wants.

Describe my antagonist. Describe how she/he/it is blocking my protagonist.

How do I establish setting? What details create the setting? What details detract from the setting?

Describe the point of view from which I've chosen to tell this story.

How do I characterize my protagonist? What details have I used to characterize she/he/it?

continued

How does my protagonist's dialogue differ from the other characters' dialogue in the story?

Describe my plot in a couple of sentences. What is the central conflict of my plot?

How many scenes do I have in my story? Could you draw a picture of each of them given the details that I've used? If not, why not? What is missing?

How are my scenes sequenced? Does the sequencing help or hurt the story?

How would you describe the mood of this story?

What details in my story help or hurt the overall narrative?

How does my story end? Do you feel satisfied by this ending?

. . . WE TALK ABOUT POETRY

Describe my structure: stanza, line length, repetition, rhyme.

Describe my speaker.

Describe the tone.

Describe the shift(s) or turn(s).

What's the relationship between title and poem?

Describe the metaphoric lens.

What is the relationship between the speaker, the audience, and the reader?

Is there a controlling metaphor or conceit? Describe it.

Given the diction, what metaphoric "leaps" are possible?

Is the poem syntactically engaging?

How do the beginning and ends of lines work?

How does the poem's "music" reinforce the meaning?

Describe the full range of sensory experience used to create images.

Describe the poem's energy.

How could this poem be extended?

How could this poem be compressed?

HOW TO READ, ANNOTATE, AND RESPOND TO AN INQUIRY DRAFT

Even though peer review has authentic roots in language arts pedagogy, the activity seemingly has become conflated with "fixing" the writing or editing for correctness. Annotating a peer's text and responding to a peer's inquiry questions is not the same process as a traditional peer review used in many language arts classrooms. Review and respond require different relational stances toward the work; one leans on correction, the other on illumination.

This is a process I explicitly teach my students. I pass out a piece of my own in-progress writing, a blog post for example or a magazine article, with four inquiry questions attached. Giving students your own writing and letting them respond is crucial to create a communal sense that we are all writers in this room, even that old chick in the corner with the reading glasses.

This may be the single largest symbolic gesture you can make toward your students—revealing your mind to them with all its errancy. And you don't have to have a blog or write articles for a magazine to share with them. Write up a reflection about a day of teaching. Write a funny story about your kids. A rant about bus duty. Anything that puts your brain on the page in the same way you've asked them to expose themselves.

The twofold gold of giving them a piece of your own writing is that you can demonstrate how they should read, annotate, and respond to an inquiry draft and also how a writer listens, accepts, and uses the information she receives from her writing group.

READING AN INQUIRY DRAFT

I tell students: First, read the writer's inquiry questions so you have in your mind which elements the writer is concerned about. Then read the piece quickly through one time to get the big picture and the gist of what the writer is trying to say in the piece. Next, read it through a second time slowly. Think about the inquiry questions as you read through the second time, marking evidence where the writer has attempted to or succeeded at executing whatever element he's asking about.

For several years, I made hard copies of writing pieces for each student in my class, which consumed a lot of paper. For each project cycle, a class of twenty-five will produce about 75–125 pages of written text during Inquiry Week. The last three years, I've distributed virtual copies of the pieces through an assignment in Google Classroom, using the "Make a Copy for Each Student" feature to distribute a single writing piece to each student in the class. They can then make their annotations individually instead of all students writing on one virtual copy, which can become confusing and messy as well as an open invitation for chicanery. When students virtually annotate, I can check the annotations, collect them in a single Google folder, and send them to the writer to read through. With this process, I'm able to measure and evaluate who is participating in the annotations and to what depth.

ANNOTATING AN INQUIRY DRAFT

Annotation has often been referred to as a "conversation" with a text, and annotating an inquiry draft should be no different. I tell students: "Think about the annotated information you would like to receive as a writer and react to your peer's text by responding in the margins with your gut responses. It's not necessary to mark grammar or usage errors. Instead, if something makes you laugh, circle it and in the margin, write *lol* or *ha ha*. If something is interesting to you, mark it and tell the writer why it's interesting in the margin. If something is confusing or contradictory, underline it, maybe write a question mark in the margin, or say, 'I don't understand this sentence.' Your goal is to interact with the text, respond to it, engage with it, keeping in mind the inquiry questions." Mark your own reactions throughout, and accompany those annotations with marginal notes. Make sure each annotation is clearly explained. There's nothing more frustrating than getting a draft back with two-thirds of the sentences underlined, but you don't know whether the reader enjoyed all those sentences or whether they should be axed.

RESPONDING TO INQUIRY QUESTIONS

After students have read through the piece twice and annotated it, they should answer the inquiry questions completely. A one- or two-word answer doesn't really help the writer and most likely will not answer the question. I encourage students to think about the questions before they respond. What does this writer really want to know about her piece?

During one project cycle, Savannah proposed a series of poems focused on a citywide arts education initiative called "Unlearn Fear + Hate." Students in our high school were encouraged to explore, through various arts discipline, this theme as it resonated with them. Here are Savannah's inquiry questions and Constance's response to them:

1. What is the message of each poem? Does it match the unlearning fear and hate theme?

   I feel that your last poem is the only one that ends with a resounding message about UNLEARNING fear/hate. Others give examples of this fear and hate learned, but the last poem forces the reader to imagine this pain caused by these learned fears/hatred (isolation, depression, rejection). The ending of this poem orders the reader to be aware of this, forces them into consciousness.

2. How could the language be more lyrical and imagistic?

   Avoid using sections heavy with rhetorical questioning. It is repetitive and can be distracting. Also, read back through your writing and stay aware of every time you TELL me a physical detail (any description that could be visual), and work on showing me that detail instead.

3. How could I make the images sharper? What other images do you wish to have seen?

   Follow the above statement.

4. Do the line breaks make sense? Punctuation? Other mechanical things? How could they be more aesthetically pleasing?

   I think your mechanics, especially line breaks, did an interesting job in setting the rhythm in which you wanted me to read these poems. Do know, though, that this is the effect. Your mechanics determine how a reader reads your material!

The greatest gift to a writer is a reader who responds with candor and clarity. Constance's specific answers to Savannah's questions gave her clear, targeted information about the four areas of concern. In question 2, Savannah asked for help with a craft issue: how could the language be more lyrical? And Constance responded with a specific technique (show, don't tell) and alerted

Savannah to the preponderance of rhetorical questions that weighed down her poetry. Notice that Savannah's third question is the same as the second question, a similarity that Constance recognizes by dittoing her response. Savannah may or may not have been aware how to sharpen her imagery and craft more lyrical language, but she knew that was an issue for which she wanted feedback. Both questions directly address that.

In Leila's response to Savannah, she echoes what Constance has said: "I think [your images] could just be a little more concrete—almost grittier, if you will. Adding in more specifics, dropping in real tiny details could sharpen them."

And Katrin's comments add to this ongoing conversation in a similar fashion: "In terms of lyricism, it always helps me to read my poems aloud as if I were reading to an audience. In terms of images, the first two poems were stronger on images. I would've loved to see specific 'monstrous' images your mind provides for you. In general, I would love to see more concrete images in each poem that illustrates what you've told us. I want to see instead of being told."

When Savannah sits down to revise, she will have an abundance of information at her fingertips to help her shape and reshape, think and rethink, fashion and refashion her poetry.

WHAT ARE SAY-BACK SESSIONS?

During Inquiry Week, the main stage is occupied by the fifteen-minute say-back sessions. Students come to class prepared with their annotated drafts of the writers under consideration for that particular day, and the days are lightning fast. Everyone is exhausted by Friday, but it's a good kind of exhaustion, like we've just raised a barn together.

The protocol is simple: The writer under consideration runs the session. She can decide if she wants readers to give her feedback on the questions one at a time or if she just wants people to jump into the say-back at any place. I start the timer. During the session, I keep time, squash sidebar conversations, keep track of who has spoken and what they've said. I don't say anything unless I absolutely have to step in.

Successful say-backs are the payoff for all those community-building activities at the beginning of the year that break down the barriers in the classroom and make it a community of students who feel safe and truly care about each other.

RULES FOR SAY-BACK SESSIONS

Here are ten rules for say-back sessions:

1. Only one student speaks at a time.

2. The say-back should directly relate to one of two things: your own experience while reading or one of the inquiry questions.

3. Focus on the writing and the inquiry, not on the writer. (Example: If a writer asked about areas of her essay that were flat, don't respond with, "You are boring." The subject is always "the writing" or "the character" or "the persona," not the writer.)

> If you are going to have students do say-back in small groups, it's probably a good idea to "fishbowl" a session for them first, so they can see what one looks like in action. You could have a group of students do the demonstration, or you might recruit a couple of your teacher friends to do one with you. At some point, you might consider recording a session on video to use with future classes.

4. Students should listen to one another, so comments are not duplicated.

5. The writer can ask questions at any time to clarify points made by another student. The writer can also make clarifications if another student asks a question or is confused about something.

6. There are no sidebar conversations, which is disrespectful to the writer, the class, and the process.

7. In large classes, everyone must offer say-back in two of the sessions each day. In smaller classes, everyone speaks once per session before anyone speaks twice.

8. Students should not provide "fixes" to the issues of the story. That's the writer's job. Providing prescriptions for the issues is not necessary unless the writer directly asks for suggestions.

9. Stay on the page. Example: Do not embark on some random discussion about the merits of socialism merely because the blog is about socialism.

10. You don't need to like a genre or even like the position the writer has taken on a subject to give her feedback on the writing. If the essay is about a hot topic, like reproductive rights, for example, be mature enough to respond to the writing only, and not color your say-back by how you feel about the subject or the writer.

TEACHING INTERPERSONAL SKILLS FOR SAY-BACK SESSIONS

These elements—speaking with civility and building from existing commentary—are two specific skills I want my students to cultivate when they offer say-back. When writers are under consideration, I want them to practice listening without ego and asking for more information, two more interpersonal skills that foster a growth mind-set for students and build success for any college or career they choose. Developing these four skills during a say-back session is great practice for student readers and student writers.

Speak with Civility

Before our first Inquiry Week, I have a discussion about how important verbal attitude is when speaking to one another. Students report that negative say-back in the right tone can be a better experience than receiving glowing say-back in the wrong tone. I encourage students to think before they speak, not just about what they are going to say, but how they are going to say it.

Language, tone, and delivery make all the difference in the world. A student who says, "I was completely confused the whole time I was reading your essay, and your conclusion is stupid" may have a valid point, but by using the word *stupid* and engaging in the hyperbole *completely confused*, he states the information in a way that will put the writer on the defensive. A better way to translate this information would be to pair the confusion with textual evidence and be specific about where the conclusion falls apart. Start with something celebratory, like, "Your essay has a lot of rich details, but I became confused with how they were organized. Also the conclusion doesn't seem to finish your thought. It feels like I, as the reader, am left hanging a bit."

Build on Existing Commentary

We also have discussions about the importance of listening to what other students say to contribute to existing commentary. Successful communicators employ this skill naturally, but it might seem awkward at first to students who have never done this.

Let's say a student has asked an inquiry question about her introduction to an argumentative essay where she has trotted out a lot of facts and statistics. Avery offers this comment: "I felt like the introduction was confusing and hard to follow because I don't know why all those facts are there. They just seem kind of stuck in there."

If students were listening to Avery, they could piggyback their own comments with these tools:

- Build from a previous comment.

  Example: *"I agree with what Avery said about the introduction being hard to follow because I didn't know if you were stating those statistics as a fact for your argument or just as a hook."*

- Contrast from a previous comment.

  Example: *"I understand what Avery said about the introduction being hard to follow, but I think you've done a great job of establishing your voice and credibility there using all those facts."*

- Clarify and qualify a previous comment.

  Example: *"To add to what Avery said about the introduction being hard to follow, I think it has less to do with all the facts and more to do with the transitions. I got confused between the second and third sentence."*

Building on existing commentary accomplishes two things: it creates a need and desire to listen to each other, and it requires the next responder to restate what a previous responder has just stated. Thus, the writer under consideration benefits from the data she receives, and the community benefits from practicing a communication skill that many adults find difficult to master.

Listen Without Ego

The writer under consideration has the responsibility of running her own session, and one of the best things she can learn to do is listen to the say-back without becoming emotionally involved. Listening with composure when any project is under consideration is a very adult skill students can begin to develop in say-back sessions.

I tell students: "Say-back does not define your worth or the worth of your writing. Maybe it's hard for you to separate the feedback on a poem written about your boyfriend and your actual boyfriend, but that's the goal. The community is commenting on the execution of your writing, not on the value of your relationships. To improve as a writer, you need to be able to separate yourself from the work, even though the work is a part of you and came from your experience."

Students need to be able to talk and listen objectively about the writing independent of the experience that inspired the writing. I ask students to listen with the writing at the center, not their ego. If they feel themselves reacting negatively or emotionally, they can remind themselves how and why this process is helping their writing and themselves as writers. Some kids are masters at artistic/writerly detachment after only a few times.

Ask for More Information

The writer under consideration should be listening and pressing his classmates if there is a point that needs explaining. I teach students a sales tactic called the "that's interesting + something else" technique. This method allows a writer to get more information from the responder by eliciting more evidence or asking for justification for their say-back. For example, a student could say, "That's interesting, tell me more," or, "That's interesting, why would you say that?," or, "That's interesting, what makes you think that?"

This technique allows the writer more opportunity to clarify and illuminate how the reader has responded and to what. The reader then can offer more evidence from the text or more support for her say-back.

SARAH'S SAY-BACK SESSION: AN EXAMPLE

Following is an example of one student's say-back session. As you read, notice how the students start with the positive and move into the inquisitive. They look at the writing critically without offering the writer prescriptions for fixing it; they are only registering what they see and hear and feel as readers. Also notice how actively Sarah participates in this session.

THE PROJECT

Sarah wanted to write a series of vignettes about her relationship with her sister, Rachel, a relationship complicated by the fact that Rachel suffers from a mental disability. Even though Rachel was middle school age, she thought and spoke and reasoned like a much younger child.

Sarah wanted to be able to capture Rachel without sentimentality, to show a regular sibling relationship in the complex scope of her sister's disability. She was irritated by her sister as any older sister would be, but she was also protective, defensive, and maternal. She wanted to strike that balance in these short vignettes.

THE INQUIRY QUESTIONS

Sarah's writer's inquiry questions showcased a clear sense of what she wanted:

1. I don't necessarily intend to present these as a collection, but instead as individual pieces. Which vignettes stand on their own and which could not?

2. How would you describe the relationship I have with my sister if you didn't know me and just read these cold?

3. Are there any sections that would benefit from more lyrical language, or is the simplicity working?

4. How would you describe my sister? In which vignette is she conveyed the least? Thanks for all the feedback!

When it was Sarah's turn for say-back, she started the inquiry by reading her questions out loud to the group. They were ready with annotated copies of her vignettes in front of them. I started the clock, and the say-back began.

THE SAY-BACK

"Wow," Rayny started. Everyone in the circle nodded in agreement. "These are really powerful."

"These pieces were beautiful, Sarah," Serena said.

"Thank you," Sarah said.

"Yeah," Gwen said. "They're very poetic. And yeah, your question about the relationship between you and Rachel, these pieces are pretty emotional, so I can see how much, I mean, I can see how complex this relationship is. But answering question 3—since there is so much emotion in here, I thought the language would be more . . . I don't know . . . it is a little dry in places."

Sarah nodded. "I thought so too. Where'd you see that?"

Gwen flipped a couple of pages. "I guess at the beginning of the second one?"

Constance jumped in. "Yeah, I think the language is a little too. . ." she searched for the right combination of words. ". . . not emotional enough or maybe not descriptive enough to get the right feeling across?"

"There's not enough detail or there's not enough poetic language?" Sarah said.

"Poetry," Rayny said. "But not like fancy words, just more stuff."

"No, not poetry, just more reflection," Serena said. "I mean, I know what is happening, but I don't know what you're thinking about Rachel in that one."

"That's what I thought too, which goes back to your first question about ones that stood out," Jamin said. "I thought the last one stood out because it. . . it's the one called 'Seizures,' it was so dark and I thought having it at the end made it seem like we were supposed to think she was going to die. But I don't know because you don't tell us."

"Oh, no," Sarah said. "I didn't intend for that. I just put them in there the way I wrote them."

"That last one was really tough to read because it was so dark," Karlee said.

"I should probably change the order then," Sarah said.

"I agree with what Karlee said because I feel like there's a lot of love and frustration here between you and Rachel and that comes across from all of these, but then when we get to 'Seizures,' it was really dark and jarring," said Meredith.

At this point the conversation goes into a lull, and I decide to step in.

"Can I read you guys a clip of this and let's think about it in light of Sarah's questions?" I said.

The group agrees and I read the vignette.

> The seizures always start slowly. She's coloring in a Disney Princess
> activity book, or watching music videos on YouTube, or stuttering out the
> latest story from the special needs classroom, or printing her name at
> the top of her math homework, or looking out the car window. Her eyes,
> those brown irises that match mine. They unfocus, fixing at some point in
> front of her that no one else can see. She'll drop anything she's holding;
> it's usually the rolling of a pencil onto the floor that catches my attention.
>
> Then the spasms start. Her hands clench and unclench, fingernails scrap-
> ing her palm. Her delicate wrists twist, flopping her hands back and forth

to some unknown rhythm. I can see the muscles in her forearm jumping if I look close enough. Her entire body shakes, the rolls of tremors building in intensity. Her mouth falls open, head lilting forward. Those long, skinny legs—they're too long for the rest of her body; Mom affectionately calls Rachel her "baby giraffe"—start kicking, lower legs jerking like the invisible hand of God is tapping her knee with a reflex hammer.

I watch her eyes. I'm trying to prepare for the day when they roll back in her head, but so far it hasn't come. Instead they stare into nothing. All I can do is wait.

Regardless of how you decide to structure say-back groups, it's best if students have read the draft they are responding to ahead of time. Trying to read a draft and figure out how to respond on the spot (with the writer sitting there) diminishes the quality of the feedback. I ask students to read their peers' drafts for homework the night before, but you might also have students read and annotate one day in class, and then share that feedback with the writer the next day.

"I liked how the last lines of all the pieces kind of wrap up the image," Joe said. "But it's not forced or anything. It kind of sounds like the last dah-duh in a song or something, like the finishing note."

"Yeah, we don't know at the end what you're waiting for, but it feels threatening, you know?" MacKenzie said.

"It doesn't sound too clichéd?" Sarah asked the group.

"No," Constance said. "It sounds final, like that's all I'm gonna say about that."

"All of your sections have that, so I thought you meant to do that," Colin said.

"I didn't really notice it until right now," Sarah said.

"You don't really linger on any details in these pieces, so sometimes I'm not sure how you feel about your sister, but I think that's why I like the last lines. It kind of helps me see how you feel about her," Joe said.

The conversation continued for a few minutes, and about fourteen minutes in, I told them there was one minute remaining. Everyone had spoken at least one time. When I called time, we moved on to the next say-back.

WEIGHING SAY-BACK DATA

The information students gain during Inquiry Week helps them move their inquiry drafts into final drafts. However, just because students have their say-back data and annotations doesn't necessarily mean they know how to use that intel effectively

Learning how to use feedback and weighing its usefulness in light of your goals for your piece of writing is a powerful skill to develop. Here are five listening and examining tips I teach to young writers on how to handle say-back data.

LISTEN FOR TEXTUAL EVIDENCE

When students employ the "That's interesting, tell me more" or "That's interesting, why do you say that?" trick, the person offering the feedback is prompted to provide evidence from the text of the issue she's addressing. If there's no textual evidence offered for the analysis, the writer may not see the need to consider this piece of feedback as credible.

For example, if a student offering say-back says, "In your inquiry question, you asked us to describe your organization. I would say your organization is a bit haphazard."

Then the writer under consideration can ask, "That's interesting. Where do you see that?"

The initial responder is then under obligation to provide some evidence of haphazardness. If the responder shrugs her shoulders and says, "I don't know. It just is," the writer may discount this piece of advice as not credible or ask the other students if they feel the same way.

However, if the responder offers four examples where the organization is, indeed, haphazard, the responder has established evidence for her claim. It's still up to the writer to decide whether she uses this feedback when revising, but it provides specific, text-bound examples of the issues about which the author has requested feedback.

EXAMINE ALL EVIDENCE EQUALLY

In some classes, one or two lead writers will emerge, and their comments will sometimes be taken as gospel by the other students. These leaders often offer clearer suggestions or more recognizable evidence with their say-back because they are articulate and can dominate the conversation.

However, I remind students that no one has all the answers, and no one's feedback is the end-all, be-all. Changing one's vision about a piece of writing just because a student you respect suggested something needed to be changed does not displace your own decision-making ability. However, if this person has valid feedback, she should be considered regardless if she's respected in the class as a leader or not.

LISTEN FOR PATTERNS

Did twenty people in the room point out that your claim is nonexistent? Then your claim is probably nonexistent. Your classmates are clearly responding to something. Perhaps you aren't signaling to them that a claim is coming. They're reading your essay and thinking, "What am I supposed to do with all this information? The claim is nonexistent!" Armed with that knowledge, the writer's job may be to create a clearer connection between the claim and the evidence.

LISTEN FOR OTHERS' BIASES

The reader's mood, for example, can influence the annotations and responses in ways that has very little to do with the merits or flaws of the writing. Some readers may have annotated while watching television, Snapchatting, painting their nails, and feeding the hamster.

I ask students: "Could the person responding to your writing be responding negatively because they're philosophically or politically opposed to the subject? Is this a reader who might not have spent much time reading and annotating?"

One student, for example, consistently made the same comment during every say-back: "This just didn't hold my attention." She said this about every piece until it became the classroom joke, but unfortunately, her credibility as a responder was diminished because her attention span was too limited to engage with the writing, not necessarily that the writing itself wasn't engaging.

However, a student might have taken her feedback to heart and looked for ways to create more engagement with the reader. If engagement was something the writer was already concerned about, then this bit of feedback may have hit the nail on the head, but if engagement wasn't an issue, taking this student's feed-

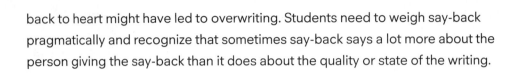

back to heart might have led to overwriting. Students need to weigh say-back pragmatically and recognize that sometimes say-back says a lot more about the person giving the say-back than it does about the quality or state of the writing.

EXAMINE YOUR OWN BIAS

Of course, this attitude can morph into artistic arrogance when a student is dismissive of all feedback because she believes her peers are lacking in the talent or acumen to give any feedback. Humility, I tell my students, is a necessary virtue for writers. The very act of writing, like golf, should keep them humble enough. Balance is the key here.

I ask students to investigate and examine their own bias. I remind them that sometimes the most oblivious reader can offer vital insight to the writer. I also remind them to consider if they are resisting a certain tidbit of say-back because if the say-back is valid, that means they have to rework something or even scrap an entire page to make the piece work. Such is the life of a writer and thinker. When new information comes to light, one must have enough integrity to say, "I see this fact, and now I must make a change."

I look at writing, specifically the writer's growth from project to project, almost like a video game where the gamer achieves more powerful levels as she adds to her command of the game. With each project, a student picks up a few more energy packs of skill and resilience and becomes a better writer by improving as a writer and cultivating the habits of a writer. One of the levels that accomplished writers eventually arrive at is how to deal with criticism and how to successfully use feedback to further their writing. Once that self-discipline begins, learning begins. And that learning is not information pointed out by a teacher, but wisdom gained through self-discovery and experience.

9

Finalizing the Work:
Final Draft, Project Reflection, and Individual Evaluation Form

Once Inquiry Week is over, the fun begins. Immediately after say-back sessions, students begin pestering me to release their annotations in our Google Classroom, so they can see what their peers have written on their drafts.

In the one to two weeks after the Inquiry Week, students still have three pieces of writing to submit to the class: the final product, a project reflection, and an Individual Evaluation Form (IEF). As they process the information they received from the say-back, they're ready to sift through the written feedback and move their product to a final-for-now state. Let's look at each of these three elements as we head down the home stretch to finalize the project cycle.

WHAT MATTERS AS STUDENTS REVISE THE FINAL PRODUCT?

As students approach the final product, I remind them they are the ultimate arbiter of the writing; however, they must learn to judge what feedback they can and cannot use in the service of the writing. Knowing if say-back is useful is about knowing one's own mind and being able to defend and concede one's writerly choices. This capacity to weigh criticism and either adopt or reject it is a critical growth point for a writer and thinker. In social science, this ability is called "agency," the ability to make up your own mind independently. Agency incorporates both self-awareness and self-control, two psychological characteristics that good writers need.

The degree to which a student can challenge himself with the feedback he's been given and improve his writing is the degree to which he believes it's possible to improve as a writer. If a student sees say-back as a reinforcement of

> You may not have a week to devote to revising, but if your students have received any feedback at all on their drafts (from you or other students), they need lessons that teach them how to consider that feedback as they revise. They also need to be held accountable to the process. When students turn in final drafts, consider having them add a note about how and why they did or didn't use feedback in their revision.

his preconceived notion that he's a bad writer, then he won't be able to use the data to move the writing forward. He's stuck. Fixed. However, when a student sees the data generated during Inquiry Week as just that—data to be used for the improvement of the piece—he can use the information to shape the expectations he already had for the piece of writing. Because he believes in himself and his writing abilities, he can use the information generated by his peers to improve the final product.

Nathan was a student who saw the say-back as information that both challenged and improved his final draft because he saw himself as a good writer. He wasn't disturbed by the say-back, even if there were areas he needed to work on, because he believed in his ability to answer the following questions:

1. What did I want this piece of writing to do in the first place?

2. What is this piece of writing in the process of becoming or shaping into?

3. In light of the previous two questions, which elements of feedback will help this writing become whatever it will eventually become?

As Nathan wrote, "The inquiry draft is helpful for me because this is really when I get to see how successful or unsuccessful my idea is. It helps me to see the places I need to work on, specifically the places that drive my story. It is definitely one of the most helpful moments in the entire process."

When students prepare to submit their final product, I ask them to consider the preceding three questions and make revisions in light of their original vision of the piece and the information they have received during annotations and say-back.

I also ask them to write a reflective argument about their growth and the entire process of this particular writing product. Let's now look at the project reflection and how it contributes to the growth of the writer and her awareness of her own process.

HOW DO STUDENTS COMPOSE THE PROJECT REFLECTION?

The project reflection accompanies the final product as an artist's statement is often displayed near a work of art. At 300–500 words, these from-the-heart personal assessments are some of the best writing my students do all year and are great examples of small, clear, insightful arguments. It's an honest, clear-eyed love letter to the class and to themselves, honoring the process they've just traversed. Having to explain their efforts requires students to self-evaluate and doing so allows them to gain perspective on their writing process, their final product, and their project management skills. Students also use this exercise to analyze and ponder on their struggles with the project and their own peaks and valleys as writers. The reflection should include the following four analyses.

AM I SATISFIED OR DISSATISFIED WITH MY FINAL PRODUCT?

In this first section, students analyze their overall satisfaction with the final product. The degrees of satisfaction about the final product can range from utter despair to delirious hallelujahs, but mostly students register a more qualified response: they are satisfied, but with reservations, or they're dissatisfied with the project as a whole, but very pleased with discrete elements of it. Sarah exemplifies this approach in her reflection of her vignette project. She writes, "I am not totally satisfied with this piece because I struggled with revision. Nothing I ever write will be able to capture my sister and our relationship. I could never do her justice. That's the trap in writing about people you care about, I guess."

All of this meta-examination is critical for the reflection, and as students consider these questions, their thinking deepens and enriches the process of ongoing inquiry. In many instances, students have a eureka moment while writing their reflection about what needs to happen to deliver more accuracy or clarity to their final product. As they write about the writing, they discover something about the writing. Wow.

HOW DID MY PIECE CHANGE FROM THE ORIGINAL VISION TO FINAL PRODUCT?

This is my favorite part of the reflection because it asks students to track the alpha and omega of an idea from inspiration to creation to publication. Many students pitch one project, then submit a slightly more augmented version in their proposal, then trot out a largely realized, but still wobbly version for Inquiry Week. When they deliver the final product, it may or may not be the thing they had originally conceived, but it has evolved. Tracking that evolution is what the reflection is all about. The ability to recognize and manage this negotiation and renegotiation of goals related to a living document is a critical tool for an independent learner, but to struggle with expressing one's own process in light of that just-finished-dance is even more powerful.

I don't know where I got this metaphor or if I invented it myself, but I use it a lot when I am conferencing with students: the car that you drive to the party isn't the party. Students often get stuck in the car—the original idea that transported them to the piece of writing that they need to write. The piece that needs to be written has the most energy, the greatest shakes. It's the party. Sometimes they don't want to get out of the car—it's safe, you know everyone in the car, and you control the radio. However, the car is just the writing prompt that brought you, but it may not be the thing that needs to be written. This section of the reflection is an opportunity for the students to describe both the car they drove to the party and the party itself.

In Victoria's process, which I shared in Chapter 2, she originally proposed a "guide to hip-hop" (the car she drove) and ended up writing a personal essay about a single hip-hop album that reflected her own scattered, disjointed upbringing (the party she arrived at). Sometimes it takes walking through the process to discover the essential thing that needed examining. Victoria writes:

> I knew when I turned my piece in for workshop I wasn't happy with it. I didn't know what voice I wanted to project onto a genre I cared so deeply about. So after workshop I decided to completely disregard the entirety of what I had worked on and single down my response to one particular article of music, the album The Miseducation of Lauryn Hill.

As I mentioned in Chapter 2, Victoria was upset about all the time wasted writing two or three different versions of what ended up being an essay, but she learned a valuable lesson about herself in the process. She writes, "These six weeks, I learned a lot about planning, never being the type of writer that thought I needed an outline." I had suggested she outline the piece at the outset of the project, but Victoria needed to discover the lessons of her own process. As a seasoned writer, I know how valuable this is. As a seasoned teacher, I know how time draining all of this is, and our time for discovery and play is increasing limited.

HOW HAVE I GROWN AS A WRITER?

In this section, I ask students to step away from the product and project at hand and analyze how they've grown as a writer. When students embark on project-based writing and they begin to see their writing talent as dynamic, something that can change, enlarge, and grow, they also grow in their identity and power as writers.

I like the way Serena described her growth in her final reflection as a senior:

> Failing as a writer is not the end—in most cases, all you have to do is hit backspace and do a bit of thinking and some trial and error. I really wish I had the maturity and levelheadedness to do that. It's so tempting to see failures and stumbles as personal shortcomings, and I'm still not to that point where I can always stare down my own mistakes enough to work through them. I feel like I am getting a little better at working through difficult parts and pieces.

This is a student who sees diligence as the missing piece in her writing tool. To understand herself in light of this awareness is an astounding reflection for any writer.

IF I ASSESSED THIS PIECE, WHAT WOULD MY SCORE BE?

In the world of project-based writing, the self-score is an interesting animal. The self-score is exactly what it sounds like: students give themselves a score on their final product based on an Individual Evaluation Form (IEF) they've designed. The argument can be made that the writer can't judge her own writing objectively because she knows the struggle of developing a sound claim for an argument or crafting just the right rhythm for poetry. The knowledge of creation does inform

No matter how a piece of writing comes to be in your class, when it's finished, having students reflect on both the product and the process is a good idea. Reflection is the tool that helps writers learn from their experiences over time. Be sure the questions you ask students to consider in their reflections make sense in the context of the work you've asked them to do. For example, if the genre was assigned, it doesn't make sense to ask students about their original vision for the work, but you might ask instead, "What was most challenging for you about writing in this genre? What was easy?"

the way one looks at his own productions, and therefore, the author may judge, not on the merit of the piece, but how difficult the journey was and how long it took to get there. But there are two reasons I have students self-score: one, self-evaluation is an important step in growing as a writer, and two, we aren't selecting and distributing Nobel Prizes for Literature here. Asking writers to score themselves using a tool they have designed and to justify their grade by that tool is asking them to look at their production dispassionately and with mature calculation, which is a valuable exercise.

It's important for the creator to judge his own work based on a tool he has crafted as he continues to develop in what I see as the whole purpose of project-based writing—cultivating writers who set their own goals and assess their own work. Of the self-scoring process, Leila wrote, "The self-score is hands down the most difficult part for me. I'm very aware that during self-score I have control of my grade. I'm also aware of the fact that I am a perfectionist, and will often be more lenient when scoring class members than when scoring myself."

Even though the personal reflection analyzes only the just-completed project, students often—even without me asking or expecting it—use the reflection to name the roadblocks in their process. They address personal indulgences as they look forward to the next project wherein they will attempt to iron out those habits as they continue on their journey.

Here's an example of Michael's most recent project, a screenplay about a delusional cult leader. Even though Michael had never read or written a screenplay before this project, he decided to read three mentor scripts and embark on his own. As you read his personal reflection, notice he doesn't see this project as a one-and-done activity, but as an ongoing project that will change and morph as he learns the screenwriting craft. During the say-back, the class encouraged him to stop writing so cautiously, so he embraced the revision time by rewriting the whole first act for the final draft.

> Starting this project cycle, I knew that I was going to have difficulty in writing a screenplay, not only because I had no experience or knowledge of writing a screenplay, but I also had a very loose idea of where I wanted to go with the story of this piece, and I still don't fully know. The first few weeks of writing reflected this. I had trouble adapting to the genre and was frustrated I was unable to convey what I wanted with it. I was not happy with the slow progress I saw and found myself losing interest. I think a lot of this sprung from my reluctance to make any mistakes or mess-ups in my first screenplay and so I held a lot back while writing, instead opting for a pretty safe, but dull compared to my original idea, of the script. However, in the days of revising, I saw the need just to push forward in the screenplay, regardless of the product, just for the sake of the story and getting it on the page, and to take your say-back advice and not hold back so as to see what I could do with writing this story in a new medium. While I wish I had more control over the way that it is written, I'm much happier with the final product of this endeavor, as I think it is much more workable and extendable into a larger piece. Overall I'm glad for choosing a screenplay this unit, because, especially in the past week, I have enjoyed doing it, and I think for both this reason and that it needs more work and developing I will continue this project into the next unit. This is a different draft from my inquiry draft. It should be read like the very beginning of the script. Thank you for reading!

HOW DO STUDENTS CREATE THE INDIVIDUAL EVALUATION FORM?

In addition to the project reflection, the other document that accompanies the final draft is the IEF. Students construct their IEF in a Google form that collects and spreadsheets all their classmates' scores and responses. Each student writer creates four declarative evaluation sentences followed by a 1–10 linear scale, with a 1 representing "no or limited evidence" and a 10 representing "abundant evidence."

Over the summer, Leila had an idea to write about a blind boy who is grieving over the death of his mother. In her proposal, she writes:

> I want to write a piece revolving around this character. While the entirety
> of the piece is going to be set in a closet, defining moments of the boy's
> life will be revealed through snapshots. I don't have the piece fully plot-
> ted out, but I do believe it will narrate two story lines—how the boy learns
> to cope with his blindness, and how he learns to cope with his mother's
> death.

However, by the time the final product arrived, Leila was much less concerned about the plot of this story as she was about the imagery she was using to describe the scenes the protagonist wouldn't have been able to see. Notice in Figure 9.1 that two of the four evaluative statements she uses in her IEF have to do with imagery and sensory detail. She clearly has an idea of what she wanted to capture with this piece of writing.

Notice how different John's IEF is for evaluating his sports blog (Figure 9.2). He's concerned about the voice and style, plus the level of analysis and the professionalism (i.e., grammatical usage and correctness in his blog posts).

The power of the IEF is threefold: students create their own form to evaluate their own work, students must identify what they see as valuable about the piece, and the form itself is minutely differentiated to the final product and the student who produced it.

FIGURE 9.1

Leila's Project One Individual Evaluation Form

The imagery in the piece is rich and vivid—it evokes emotion and atmosphere.

No Evidence   **Abundant Evidence**

1	2	3	4	5	6	7	8	9	10
O	O	O	O	O	O	O	O	O	O

The protagonist is relatable, even though he has a disability none of us have experienced. You are able to experience the world in a similar manner to how he would.

No Evidence   **Abundant Evidence**

1	2	3	4	5	6	7	8	9	10
O	O	O	O	O	O	O	O	O	O

The relationship between the characters is developed and enhanced through dialogue exchanges and interactions.

No Evidence   **Abundant Evidence**

1	2	3	4	5	6	7	8	9	10
O	O	O	O	O	O	O	O	O	O

The concepts in the piece, including the language through which it is told, challenge your perception of sight and visual images.

No Evidence   **Abundant Evidence**

1	2	3	4	5	6	7	8	9	10
O	O	O	O	O	O	O	O	O	O

SUMMARY OF EVIDENCE:

FIGURE 9.2

John's Project Three Individual Evaluation Form

The analysis displays a mature and refined understanding of the material, in order to make the narrator reliable.

No Evidence									Abundant Evidence
1	2	3	4	5	6	7	8	9	10
O	O	O	O	O	O	O	O	O	O

The voice in these posts is casual and clear, in order to make the writing relatable and easy to understand for an informed audience.

No Evidence									Abundant Evidence
1	2	3	4	5	6	7	8	9	10
O	O	O	O	O	O	O	O	O	O

The style of writing is unique and offers fresh input, in order to differentiate it from similar works.

No Evidence									Abundant Evidence
1	2	3	4	5	6	7	8	9	10
O	O	O	O	O	O	O	O	O	O

The writing itself would fit well in a blog, and there are few or no grammatical or spelling errors throughout, in order to build cohesiveness.

No Evidence									Abundant Evidence
1	2	3	4	5	6	7	8	9	10
O	O	O	O	O	O	O	O	O	O

EVIDENCE OF SCORE:

HOW DO PRODUCT GOALS AND INQUIRY QUESTIONS LEAD TO THE INDIVIDUAL EVALUATION FORM?

It's important to take a moment here to discuss the connection between the four product-specific goals, the inquiry questions, and the IEF. George Hillocks' research (1995) indicates that inquiry is naturally at the core of the impulse to write, and that by teaching students strategies for inquiry, we teach them to interpret, evaluate, and test their own writing. As the project advances, that is, as the student writes and thinks, puts ideas down in writing, then crosses out the writing in favor of better writing and rearranges her previous assumptions about the original idea, she exchanges her initial goals for the more fully realized qualities that her writing is now showcasing. The writing develops, emerges, evolves, as Lamott (1994) pointed out, "like a Polaroid" (32). The reflective chain—goals to inquiry questions to IEF—creates a system of evaluation that both sustains the project and engages the writer in perpetual inquiry while the project grows and emerges.

Finalizing the IEF, then, is one of the easiest steps to the project-based writing flow. Students shouldn't see the IEF as the end of the line for the piece of writing, but as one more weigh station to get feedback from their peers and teachers. To define categories that will assess the final product, students first look at their product goals and inquiry questions.

In Chapter 6 and Chapter 8, we looked at Jenna's goals and then her inquiry questions. Let's look at how those align (or don't) with the categories she selected for her final evaluation form.

If you currently are using teacher-created rubrics, you might consider letting each student create one or two additional rubric categories for evaluation on their individual pieces of writing. Students could submit these with their final drafts, and the evaluation categories would be based on some aspect of the writing they feel they would like to be evaluated on. The process of deciding what those categories will be is a rich metacognitive exercise.

FIGURE 9.3

The Path of Inquiry

Goal Statements	Inquiry Questions	Individual Evaluation Categories
The pacing in my short story should be smooth in order to keep the reader's attention and move the story forward.	How did the pacing help or hurt the story? Are there any parts that are too fast or too slow that cause the reader to be taken out of the story?	The pacing of the story makes it readable and fully developed so that it cohesively binds the events of the story
The voice in my short story should be unique and aware in order to make a connection between the reader and the story.	How would you describe the voice of the narrator telling the story?	The plot line is clear and the story comes together in a vivid and defined way.
The world building in my short story should be clear and play along with the events in the story in order to create a realistic and developed plot.	In what way was the world that the story takes place in developed and how did that help the reader to accept the events within the story?	The style within the piece is consistent and evident throughout the piece and allows for an interesting and hooking story.
The syntax within my short story should be coherent and understandable in order to create a readable and good-sounding piece.	How was Sophie characterized? Was there enough characterization for Sophie being the protagonist?	The protagonist is clearly characterized with elements of imagination and motive in the piece.

Notice as her awareness of her product grows, the language she uses to assess and evaluate her writing becomes sharper and targeted to the qualities of the writing she wants to see in her final product. Notice she is still interested in gaining feedback on pacing and characterization, but world building and voice of the narrator have been supplanted and substituted for categories involving plot and style.

As the original goals naturally morph into the inquiry questions, the inquiry questions now also shape the final evaluation categories by which the project will be assessed. This evaluation tool represents a coda to the original goals students made six weeks earlier. Kynnadie, a senior in my class, sums up this struggle perfectly:

> I don't know what I want from a piece until I've written it. For this last six weeks, I put theme *as a goal, and after I'd written the piece I realized I cared less about theme than I did my voice and cohesion of the pieces together. I cared more that the pieces worked together and that my voice carried throughout all of the pieces.*

Kynnadie's awareness is at the heart of what is crucial about all writing instruction—allowing students to grope along, even when they're not sure what they want to say or how to say it, while supporting them with a framework that allows for the evolution. When they start, students are in that dark cave with their head covered with a bag while they write the first draft blindly, but then take the bag off and drag the creation out into the light to see what they've built. Students need to be able to judge what the piece is already doing well and what still needs adjustments. The chain of inquiry helps them do that.

HOW DOES A FINAL EVALUATION SUPPORT FAILURE?

Last year, Ruby emailed me a question after her say-back session. "When I write something I think is good, the class think it's bad. When I write something I think is crap, everyone loves it. Do I change it for an audience or do I keep it for me? How do I decide good criticism from bad criticism?"

Part of the issue, I wrote to Ruby later, was that she was thinking of her work in terms of "good" and "bad," which is an unhealthy, maybe even dangerous, predisposition to bring to bear on a piece of writing in process. When students think of their work in terms of "this is good" or "this is bad," the growth inherent in the process is tied to some loosely defined, subjective value. What is goodness and badness in terms of writing? I like to think instead of writing as "successful" or "not successful" in terms of their own progressively clarified goals for the piece.

My husband wrote a short story titled "Visions," and he gave it to me and his writing buddy, Chris, to read. Both of us weighed in with criticism of the main character's development and the main plot device. Paul listened to us patiently, but then decided he liked the story exactly as it was. He then proceeded to send it out to several short story contests, and lo and behold, he won two of them.

Who was right about this piece of writing? Chris and me or Paul? Is winning a contest (or two) an indicator of value? If he had listened to us, would the piece have been as successful as it was? Maybe it would have been more successful or maybe not.

In the real world of writing, writing is successful if it accomplishes the job that the writer intended it to accomplish. Lab reports and legal briefings and technical manuals have different aims than love letters or fan fiction or movie scripts, but in one area they are all the same: One person is writing to communicate to another person who is reading. Therefore, rather than ask, "Is this any good?" ask, "Does this piece do the work I laid out for it to do? Have I communicated the message? Have I captured the moment? Have I told my story? Does this achieve my purpose?"

Only the writer can answer these questions.

In a typical English class, the writing is assigned, then written, then assessed. Boom. End of story. There are very few opportunities for extended composing or writing about the writing or writing around the writing or writing in service of the writing, other than perhaps an isolated prewriting activity and a single draft. In Applebee and Langer's study (2011), out of 8,542 assignments given to 138 students, only 19 percent of the assignments asked students to write more than a paragraph, and 81 percent of the assignments were fill-in-the-blank, short-answer, or copying directly from a teacher. This is not thinking or writing.

Because project-based writing requires metawriting throughout the whole process, students are writing five smaller pieces (pitch, proposal, rubric, inquiry draft, and reflection) in support of and in addition to the product being managed to publication. In a single project cycle, a student in a classroom using a fully implemented project-based writing curriculum will write a conservative 3,600 words, which adds up to 21,600 words or eighty-six pages over the course of an academic year. (Word counts vary depending on the genre and form, obviously, but the point is, students are writing a lot.)

Why is this important? Because writing begets writing. The more a student writes, the better she becomes at writing. As with any skill, the necessary muscles for producing a piece of writing for an audience are forged by repetition.

We are not teaching students to be Shakespeare, unless, of course, they want to be Shakespeare. Those students destined to be Shakespeare will no doubt arrive at their lot regardless (or because of) the hooks sunk into them by crones like me. Instead, we are teaching students to become thinkers and communicators, to understand their own minds, and to grow their powers of communication to express themselves with all the clarity at their disposal. And they need lots and lots and lots of practice to do this.

In this light, project-based writing and specifically the IEF are critical to the development of a mind composing, failing, succeeding, and evaluating. The ultimate takeaway from this book, then, is not about mastery, but about failure. About making a space for failure in our classrooms and supporting kids as they face the failures necessary to forge a critical mind.

Students need to learn how to make choices, but then also be allowed to make mistakes. How to manage their time and fail at it. How to take on a project and learn from its successes and its failures. And the IEF creates a way for students to continue to learn about their process and their abilities without the defeat of an end-all, be-all grade that determines their worth as a writer or their grade for an entire course.

Just giving students voice and choice is not enough. The goal is to teach them how to fail, not to perpetuate defeat, but as a way to gather intel about themselves as learners. It's giving them confidence by showing them how to manage the large project of writing, how to set goals, and ultimately, how to evaluate and judge for themselves the products of their own minds.

10

Revealing the Work:
Community Score and 4P

A s a writer, I can think of no better enticement to a student than to see his work validated by a living, breathing audience. I say validated; some would say exposed, but the goal is the same: to get their words, their thoughts, their stories, *out there*.

This is the goal of 4P, to reveal the writing to an audience outside the classroom through (1) performance, (2) presentation, (3) production, or (4) publication. However, before students seek a home for their work, they have one more opportunity to gain additional feedback and improve it through a process called "Community Score."

Structured collaboration is one of the core elements of all project-based learning, and in project-based writing, even though students are pursuing a singular independent project, they're dependent on their writing peers to provide essential support at every step of the flow. The Community Score is the final formative data collection for my students. From the introduction of the writing idea in pitch and proposal to the inquiry stage of the first draft, students are bouncing ideas off their peers, and their peers are bouncing right back.

HOW DO STUDENTS EVALUATE EACH OTHER'S PROJECTS IN COMMUNITY SCORE?

The Community Score serves two purposes: to gain more formative data for the writer and to create community accountability to ensure high-quality final products. In short, the Community Score is where students assess one another's final product using each student's own evaluation tool and reflection. These three documents—the final product, the project reflection, and the Individual Evaluation Form—are posted in Google Classroom. The process takes about three days of class time reading and responding for the whole class. There's lots of coffee involved.

There is a palpable energy and anticipation in the room on Community Score days, but also a seriousness as each student undertakes her task. It's been two weeks or so since the class saw the inquiry draft, so students approach the final product with a "wonder how this piece turned out" attention. The three days of scoring have the feeling of a big ta-da!

When scoring, each student reads the accompanying project reflection first, then studies the accompanying individual evaluation tool, then reads the final product. After that, the instructions for the process are simple. Students are asked only to judge the piece based on the four categories the student writer has indicated. Each student scores the piece from 1 to 10 on each of the four categories the writer has deemed essential for the success of this product. In addition, each student provides a short constructed response (50–75 words) with evidence that supports her score. All of these comments and scores are collected in a Google form and then given to the student writer on the last day of the project cycle.

As with the pitching and say-back sessions, if you don't have this much class time to devote to this part of the project cycle, consider breaking students into small groups for final evaluations. The evaluation form can also be truncated, and you can group students who are writing in the same form or genre together.

Here are some sample responses Jenna received regarding the short story she wrote about a little girl with a monster living under her bed, which reveals an interesting theme about the nature of youth and innocence. As you saw in the last chapter, in her Individual Evaluation Form, she selects the categories of pacing, style, characterization, and plot for students to evaluate and respond:

Responder #1

Sophie is far more developed than she was in the inquiry draft. I love all of the little details about how she redecorated her room, and searched for Cerdra through her books—it all adds up and contributes to her character. The plot is well defined, but there are some subplots I'm still confused about—mainly that of her father. The family moved for work,

yet he still has to travel? He also was staying with a friend—is this to say
he is cheating on his wife? I liked the style—it was consistent through-
out. I didn't see an issue with the pacing. Again, my only comment
would be the setup with the father, by having him appear, and the little
follow-through as he was mentioned in passing. But it was very balanced
throughout. Great concept—and nice job!

Notice this reader responded to all of Jenna's concerns along with additional textual evidence. In addition, this reader gave Jenna 38/40 on her Individual Evaluation Form.

Here's another sample from the same class:

Responder #2
I think you do a good job with Sophie as a character. My heart breaks
at the end for her. The plotline makes sense and it starts at a clear
beginning and resolves itself efficiently. The writing style is not only con-
sistent—but also interesting. It's got children's fiction aspects to it, but it's
not that. There wasn't any point in the story where I thought it was going
too fast or slow—so pacing is a plus.

This reader addresses all four concerns, but with less evidence and depth, and scored Jenna's piece at 39/40.

Google forms makes this process super easy; once students create their form, they transfer ownership of it to me, which allows me to post the form to our Google Classroom and allows me to observe, control, and harvest the results. From the Google form, I can create a spreadsheet, and using the averaging tools embedded in Google Sheets, average the individual categories as well as the overall score.

I participate in the Community Score as well, using the same Individual Evaluation Form, but my score is not averaged in with the class and is weighted as a summative score. The Community Score (formative assessment), the writer's self-score (formative assessment), and the teacher's score (summative assessment) are recorded as three different grades for the student's final product in the gradebook.

In addition, all twenty-four students responded with a small paragraph that justified the score they awarded the piece. Jenna will be given this single document that collects all twenty-four constructed responses along with the collected data from the Google form graphing how students scored her piece in each of the four categories.

I can't think of any traditional teacher-student assessment exchange that meets the kind of accountability and engagement level the Community Score offers. Although the 4P creates an external incentive for students to perform, the Community Score becomes a mini performance of its own. Sarah said, of the process, "The degree of success of a writing project, at least from my perspective, is a combination of its reception among peers/out in the world, and the writer's personal satisfaction. This is reflected in the combination of the Community Score and the self-score. Both are important in the project cycle."

Although peer grading has its detractors, I firmly believe in it for several reasons. Writing is about communicating with an audience. Without an audience, the writing loses its focus. Writing for an audience of one (me) does not create the kind of accountability real writing for a wider audience creates. All students in the project-based writing class submit their work to be judged by a wider writing community of contests, editors, publishers, and performance audiences, such as the YouTube or Vimeo public, so revealing their final product first to a smaller, more supportive audience of their own peers is a good way to measure the success of the project prior to sending it out, as well as generating more feedback for future improvement.

If you're not comfortable with students scoring each other's work, for whatever reason, they can still give each other written (or even verbal) feedback on the specific issues each writer identifies for evaluation on his project. As you can see from these examples, the feedback itself is rich and detailed, and as students respond to the writing of others, they can't help but learn more about the craft of writing itself.

HOW DO STUDENTS GO PUBLIC WITH THEIR PROJECTS?

After students receive Community Score feedback, they continue to tweak the piece of writing. The pieces miraculously get better even beyond the final product stage because students continue to either pare down or sharpen up the pieces for an audience outside our classroom.

The 4P requirement for project-based writing is the only step in the flow that doesn't have to be completed by the end of the project cycle. In other words, students have the entire semester to find a 4P home for their work. December and May are big 4P months in my classroom because those students who haven't found a home for their pieces are scurrying to submit.

Although I encourage them to submit within a month of completion, some students get busy with their next project and put off this step, telling themselves they have to find the "perfect" 4P home. They are not required to publish the piece but only to submit it somewhere seeking publication (although many are published), whereas if they perform, produce, or present, students are required to have finished the performance, production, or presentation by the deadline.

For the projects to have any value at all, there must be something demanded of students beyond a grade. The stakes, like the inspiration, must be rooted in the gut. And honestly, if we are designing our curriculum to follow the path of real writers, then the agony and the ecstasy of a real audience is a necessity.

Even though students stated a 4P goal in their pitch and proposal, often the final product has evolved or transformed to the point where their initial 4P goal is either unattainable or unfit, and they must research and look for another home. And sometimes they want to shoot for a higher-stake (or lower-stake) venue depending on how the final project turned out.

A low-stakes outlet might be publishing an essay on a personal blog or our classroom blog; a high-stakes outlet might be reading a short story at a Friday night coffee house open mic. Depending on the student, I suggest they shoot for three high-stakes venues and two low-stakes venues over the course of an academic year, but that's not a hard-and-fast rule, just a suggestion I make to students hanging out in their comfort zone. What constitutes a low-stakes venue to one student might be a nerve-wracking high-stakes venue to another.

To give you an idea of the range of places where my students have found 4P homes, let's look at a few of their projects. For her first three projects, Gwen wrote poetry, a short story, and a series of satirical blog posts about being one of Santa's elves at the mall. She performed her poetry at a local open mic feature called Teen Howl; she submitted her short story to Scholastic Art & Writing Awards (and won a Gold Key); and she created her own WordPress blog to post online.

Other students have submitted their work to our school's own literary magazine, *The Laurel*, as well as *Teen Ink*, and their own Tumblr blogs. Two of my students researched and discovered a first-time screenwriter's competition for high school students offered by the American Movie Awards, and they both decided to enter feature length scripts. Joe wrote a humorous romp entitled *McConaughey Goes to High School* and Serena wrote a dark edgy piece called *The Earnest Inner Circle* about a group of small town boys obsessed with black metal who plan a murder.

When students write smaller forms, like poetry and vignettes, I don't require they submit and publish all of them, but only a selected representation of the whole project. When Sarah wrote a series of vignettes about different seasons, she selected and submitted "Snowy Spring Blossoms," the only one she thought was strong enough to be considered for the *Amazing Kids Magazine* website (http://mag. amazing-kids.org/non-fiction/stories/ snowy-spring-blossoms/). The vignette was published there as well as on *Teen Ink* (www.teenink.com/nonfiction/ personal_experience/article/922001/ Snowy-Spring-Blossoms/).

I have many students who write college essays and "submit" them to Common App or with their college application, which satisfies the requirement of a real-world audience looking at their work.

Sometimes students will hit the trifecta and find a venue that has multiple outlets. For example, our high school hosts an arts night each semester where

If you don't want to require all your students to take their writing out of the classroom and into the world, you might invite them to consider a wider audience, such as a club or local school board or a business that might benefit from their work. Just having information available on performance, publishing, production, and presentation opportunities might be enough to get some students headed in that direction (and a little encouragement wouldn't hurt either). And almost certainly, if one students gets up the courage to try it, others will follow.

dancers, artists, pianists, and writers perform. For my writers who participate, their work is published in the program, which is distributed at the event. They also read their work (performance), which is then videoed by our school district (production) and showcased on a local cable access channel: published, performed, and produced in a single sweep.

Let's break down some more 4P possibilities for student writers, and then we'll consider a few additional possibilities for going public through online communities.

PUBLICATION

Most of my students choose this avenue for their writing because it is somewhat low stakes. I like it because students get experience submitting for publications, which has numerous tangential lessons, including close reading of submission guidelines and preparing their manuscripts with formatting dependent on those guidelines. A lot of students don't realize there are a variety of ways to format manuscripts outside of MLA or APA. In fact, most students don't recognize the industry side of writing until they get to college.

Researching a possible venue for an article or essay, studying submission guidelines, and actually submitting their work to a contest or a publication is great training for budding writers. I introduce them to websites such as New Pages (www.newpages.com/magazines), Writer's Digest (www.writersdigest. com), and *Poets & Writers* (www.pw.org), which has a searchable index for numerous possible venues as well as a database of articles on fiction, poetry, and nonfiction craft issues. Students have also submitted their work to contests like Scholastic Art & Writing and the National Council of Teachers of English Norman Mailer contest, which award, as part of their prize packages, the chance to be published. There are also local contests such as those sponsored by the Kentucky Poetry Society, which publishes the winners in their literary magazine.

Another indirect benefit of seeking publishing outlets is that students begin to read online literary magazines searching for potential submission spots. I tell them not to send their writing like a plague of locusts out upon the land, but to make a smart, targeted, well-researched submission. One of the first things I ask students when they are considering submitting to a venue is: "Have you read their publications to know what kinds of work they publish?" Some online venues have hyperlinked back copies or provide free sample copies.

Another lesson of submission for publication is the soft skill of fortitude. Again let me state that the goal of 4P is not to get published, but merely to submit the piece for publishing, but there is merit and value in getting that first rejection slip and sharing it with the class. There's great growth from sending something out into the world, having it rejected, and yet remaining steadfast in the belief of its worth. We have discussions of how Rowling, Gaiman, and Melville were rejected numerous times. I have famous rejection letters of Andy Warhol and Sylvia Plath on the wall of my classroom. I share my own rejection letters with them.

But students don't have to submit their work to a literary magazine to meet the requirement of submitting for publication—they can choose a school, local, or regional newspaper or a citywide publication or circular (Figure 10.1). Some students are industrious enough to self-publish their work and distribute it at school, which would count as both publication and production.

FIGURE 10.1

Publishing Outlets for Teens

- *Amazing Kids Magazine* (http://mag.amazing-kids.org/) is an online publication that features work by both middle grade and teen writers. They also host interviews with mentor writers and have monthly writing contests.

- The *Claremont Review* (www.theclaremontreview.ca/) publishes young writers and artists, aged thirteen to nineteen, from anywhere in the English-speaking world. Twice yearly, they accept fiction, poetry, drama, graphic art, and photography.

- *Hanging Loose Magazine* (http://hangingloosepress.com/current.html), a division of Hanging Loose Press, supports and publishes teen writers in their monthly magazine. They accept poetry and prose from high school students and will offer feedback and editorial advice if requested. If work is accepted, writers are paid a small stipend and receive two copies of the magazine wherein their work appears.

- *Rookie* magazine (www.rookiemag.com/) is a publication especially for teen girls, and I love the funky graphics of this site, which posts writing and art from their readers. Rookie also hosts over twenty categories of posts from "eye candy" to "you asked it" sections with writing on music, style, clothes, and fashion.

continued

- Stone Soup (https://stonesoup.com/) has been around for more than forty years and is now available in both print and web versions. The readers and writers of this magazine are fourteen years or younger, so only freshmen writers might want to pursue a publishing spot with this publication.

- Teen Ink (www.teenink.com) has been around since 1989, offering teen writers publishing opportunities. Teen Ink considers submissions for their online and print magazine, as well. Teen Ink also provides feedback on novels.

- Teen Lit (www.teenlit.com) distributes free books to teens in exchange for a review that is edited and then published on their site. They also publish short stories, poetry, and essays on their site and host a discussion board, a writing community, and a treasure trove of writing links for craft and inspiration.

- *VOYA*, or *Voice of Youth Advocates* magazine (http://voyamagazine.com/), is a journal that promotes young adult literature and reading. The magazine invites teen writers to contribute to the magazine through poetry and art contests, as a book reviewer, or by submitting a manuscript for the Notes from the Teenage Underground column.

- YARN, or Young Adult Review Network (http://yareview.net/), is an online literary journal that publishes fiction, poetry, and essays for young adult readers, written by established authors and teen writers.

PERFORMANCE

My poets, specifically those who are spoken word and slam poets, are definitely drawn to this category. In Lexington, we are fortunate to have a vibrant and supportive writing community, and there are numerous opportunities throughout the year for students to perform their work. Currently, four monthly open mic opportunities in town welcome teens, and many others are held annually, such as the open mic at the Kentucky Women Writers Conference.

Coffee houses and open mics are great venues for performances, but you can also host a spoken word performance during lunch in the cafeteria, after school, during club meetings, or even at a public speaking area at a local park. Depending on their genre and form, students could read an essay as part of a local club-sponsored speech series or at a church youth group or summer camp group.

PRESENTATION

My students use this category less often, but I have had students in the past who presented their essays, speeches, and findings to community and school clubs, specifically local historical societies, civic groups, nursing homes, agricultural cooperatives, and lifestyle clubs, like homemaker and artists' groups. One student presented her informational blog on raising sheep to her 4-H club. Another group of students presented different oral histories based on interviews of their grandparents to a local history club, an activity that originated in their social studies class and spilled over into my English class.

Often presentations are of the informational/explanatory genre and are connected to the interest of the club or the audience. I also allow students to use presentations to other classes if the other teacher is OK with that. Students have completed college entrance exams as projects and "presented" them with their college applications. These have been some of the most instructive projects because of the high stakes riding on college admission.

PRODUCTION

Students who are more tech savvy may want to produce their work as a podcast, using their personal blog, or on their YouTube channel as a quasi-TED talk, a short film, a table read, or a piece of spoken word. One student spent a project cycle working on a script for a graphic novel and then gave it to some friends of his (not in my class) who were illustrators to produce a comic book. Students who write dramatic scripts, either for the screen or the stage, are often drawn to this category. With the proliferation of video capacity on cell phones and free editing software, students can use this as an easy way to gain access to a greater audience with a little more work. Sometimes this category becomes collaborative if they ask their peers to read parts or play characters for screen or stage plays.

ONLINE WRITING COMMUNITIES

Another way students can reveal their work to the world is to join an online writing community. In these communities, participants submit their pieces for discussion and ranking by other members.

If students are old enough and responsible enough to have a Facebook page, they also may enjoy joining online writing communities. Several of my students have used one or more of the following to publish their work:

- Figment (http://figment.com/) has a lot of bells and whistles including a blog called "The Daily Fig," which features posts about craft, inspiration, plotting, manuscript formatting, and much more. There are also multiple forums and a feature called "Figment Chats" where members can chat with published authors and writers.

- Go Teen Writers (http://goteenwriters.blogspot.com/) has a community that is supportive and very helpful with a seriously well-stocked archive of craft articles about plot, characters, point of view, and much more. Maintained by young adult authors Stephanie Morrill, Jill Williamson, and Shannon Dittemore, the site is well designed and generous with resources for teen writers.

- Scribophile (www.scribophile.com/) is less a social media site than it is an online workshop where community members share their work to get and give feedback as well as trade information about writing.

- Wattpad (https://www.wattpad.com/home) is a streamlined social media site for writers and readers. If students create a profile, they can post chapters of their novels and read the work of other writers from more than twenty different genres for free.

- Writer's Café (www.writerscafe.org) is a similar social media site that hosts a blog and has a neat publishing tab with a searchable database of literary magazines and writing contests.

- Write the World (https://writetheworld.com/) is a global, nonprofit organization that works with teachers and student writers all over the world. They offer writing groups for peer review as well as competitions, writing prompts, and expert feedback. This site also provides resources, writing prompts, and lessons for teachers of creative writing.

11

The Big Picture:
Terms, Practices, Structures, Standards, and Grading

So that's it. The end of the trail. Or Montana, for all you *Lonesome Dove* fans. In Chapter 2, I gave you a brief tour of one student's project cycle, then in Chapters 4 through 10, I described the seven steps of project-based writing, breaking down each step bit by bit. We've trekked through the whole framework, but I know you still have lots of questions.

In this chapter, let's widen the angle a bit to get a few big picture views of this framework. First, I'll offer some explanations of important terms and explain the perennial practices of the project-based writing system, as well as its infrastructure and structure. And then finally, we'll turn our attention to covering standards and dealing with grades.

FOUR PROJECT-BASED WRITING TERMS: PROCESS, PRODUCT, PROJECT, AND PRACTICE

First of all, there are four distinct terms we use in the project-based writing system, each distinct and not interchangeable with one another. I teach students these terms explicitly, so everyone understands what each term means when we discuss a student's processes, products, projects, and practices.

STUDENT PROCESSES

In my classroom, we use the term *process* to describe the method and manner of writing and reading that is unique to the student. The process describes how and why students work—how they read, write, manage, talk, listen, argue, live. Their processes may be functional or dysfunctional or somewhere in between, but they're as unique as the students themselves, born from their childhoods, their experiences, their beliefs and values about themselves and the world. A student's process, as a mechanism by which he manages life, is idiosyncratic and extremely personal.

In project-based writing, I want to do everything I can to protect and yet make students aware of their own processes. Instead of supplanting their processes with an artificial one of my own or forcing a one-size-fits-all process on everyone, I want students, through the supports offered by the project-based framework, to see, maybe for the first time, how they work, how they process information, how the habits they have unwittingly maintained might be holding them back or might be the key to their success.

Even though creative processes often follow the same pattern (preparation, incubation, illumination, verification), each of us have our characteristic methods of creation. In this aspect, teachers could do well to heed a page from Hippocrates and "first, do no harm."

STUDENT PRODUCTS

My students and I use the term *product* to describe the finished artifact or creation born from a student's process and delivered by the end of the project cycle. In my class, students will create six unique products, which are not to be confused with the discrete deliverables that support the project cycle, such as the proposal, goals, schedule, library, inquiry draft, and reflection. The product is the culmination of the idea that students first envision and subsequently build during the course of a single project. The product is the pot born on the potter's wheel and fired in the kiln, the ultimate Art Thing students conceive, create, and eventually set free into the world.

STUDENT PROJECTS

The term *project* describes the whole scheme and plan that supports the production of the product. A project encompasses all the time-dependent tasks by which a student delivers a product. I define a project cycle as the period of time that starts when a student pitches her idea to the community and ends when she delivers the finished product to an outside-the-classroom audience.

STUDENT PRACTICES

Student practices are those four practices I seek to cultivate that will benefit my students far into the future: reading, writing, project management, and community engagement. I will discuss these individually in the next section of this chapter, but for now, I define a student *practice* as the ongoing exercise and training of a set of skills for the express purpose of improving those skills.

I referred earlier to yoga as an example of a practice. Yoga practitioners call it a "practice" because their goal is not to arrive at a terminus or pronounce a mastery over it. Instead, they recognize the illusory nature of mastery and concentrate on getting better at traversing the path they're on. So much of yoga practice is about being present and listening to one's own body, just as writing and reading are about being present and listening to one's own mind. Learning how to manage time and tasks and learning how to engage in a community is a similar practice, where one learns a little more every day (and some days regresses).

Another reason to distinguish these activities as "practices" is that anyone, anywhere can start right where he is practicing the art of writing, reading, project management, and community engagement. The practice naturally fits the practitioner. In yoga, some people are more flexible than others, some can hold challenging poses because they have greater upper body strength, but we're all practicing the same thing right where we are with the skills and the abilities and the will we have brought to the mat. Reading and writing are similar in this respect. In a project-based classroom, the four perennial practices serve the student in the same way.

PROJECT-BASED INFRASTRUCTURE: FOUR PERENNIAL PRACTICES

Writing, reading, community engagement, and project management are the four perennial practices that serve as the practical and theoretical "undergirding" of the whole instructional framework. These practices are rigorous, continuous, and transportable from my class to the rest of a student's life and further academic career. More than any other standard students may meet or exceed in my classroom, I want them to develop a lifelong practice in reading and writing, to coexist productively and successfully in groups, and to have the management skills to carry out large projects. To those ends, the four perennial practices I have discussed throughout the first ten chapters establish the substructure for all the projects students will undertake.

Figure 11.1 is a graphic representation of the infrastructure on which all student projects are conceived, built, and delivered. Notice the four practices are ongoing and independent of any specific project, yet supportive of all projects a student might undertake.

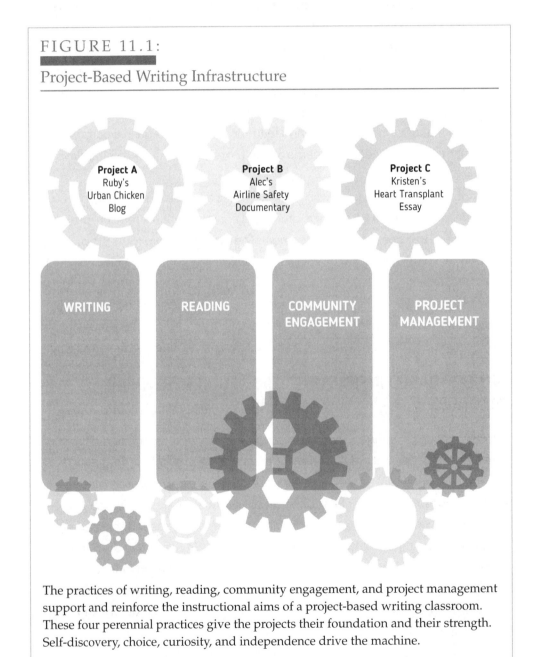

FIGURE 11.1:

Project-Based Writing Infrastructure

The practices of writing, reading, community engagement, and project management support and reinforce the instructional aims of a project-based writing classroom. These four perennial practices give the projects their foundation and their strength. Self-discovery, choice, curiosity, and independence drive the machine.

PERENNIAL PRACTICE NUMBER ONE: WRITING

Writing is the queen of all practices because from it and through it all other skills and competencies flow. Out of the writing practice, students discover their ideas, but they will also write their proposals, inquiry drafts, reflections, and final products. Students maintain a writing practice as both a depository of ideas and a record of their ongoing inquiry. The self-designed writing practice supports their projects but can be independent of them as well. They design the terms of this writing practice based on data from a writing practice questionnaire and recommendations from me. I like to think of this practice and its physical manifestation (a composition notebook, a large Google doc, a series of Evernote notes, among others) as the source of all ideas as well as a bible of drafts and the location of all research and reflection that a student might produce throughout the whole year.

PERENNIAL PRACTICE NUMBER TWO: READING

Out of the reading practice, students select and read mentor texts that support their specific project genre, but they will also read a variety of craft essays on grammar, technique, and methodology as well, which supports all writing, not just writing that is project-specific. The reading is 75 percent student selected based on the perceived requirements of the project, and 25 percent teacher directed based on the formative data the teacher gathers during conferences. Students maintain a self-designed reading practice throughout the year that supports their projects. They design the terms of this reading practice based on data from a reading practice questionnaire and recommendations from me. This practice supports and strengthens their own reading abilities and their own project needs. This practice and its physical manifestation, the project library, are the source of all reading practice, including reading for research, reading for pleasure, reading for discovery, reading text models, and reading for craft instruction that a student might engage in throughout the whole year.

PERENNIAL PRACTICE NUMBER THREE: COMMUNITY ENGAGEMENT

Out of the community engagement practice, students engage and partici-pate in an active, functional, supportive writer's community, wherein they give and receive product-specific data to other vested members of the community throughout the project cycle. While doing this, they develop a big bag of inter-personal skills and tricks that will serve them for a lifetime, not only listening and speaking skills, but competencies in group negotiations and self-management. In addition to the personal growth and self-discovery that benefit a student indi-vidually, she also cultivates the skills necessary to be a civil, responsible, and contributing member of a supportive writing community.

PERENNIAL PRACTICE NUMBER FOUR: PROJECT MANAGEMENT

And finally out of the project-management practice, students gain independence and agency as they cultivate the ability to discover, initiate, problem-solve, and evaluate their own intellectual creations. To usher into life future writing, inven-tions, works of art, or scientific breakthroughs, students learn to conceive, execute, manage, and complete projects during the course of a year through practicing the seven steps of the project-based management framework.

Any good project management system is about efficiency and effective-ness. But pairing that with inspiration and creation gives students a way to manage themselves within a boundary of time and task. As a writer, I know that structure, boundaries, and the accountability of a deadline actually engendered freedom and creativity in me.

This is the paradox of creativity. My students have the ability to choose their own projects, make decisions, take action, and produce original work not in spite of but because they are working in a community system that holds them accountable. No conflict exists between creativity and a framework because it supports rather than defeats the efficient production of ideas. Writing, or any cre-ative production, flourishes in a system of expectations. Instead of being trapped in the stranglehold of perfectionism, for example, deadlines push us to finish a project.

PROJECT-BASED STRUCTURE: THE SEVEN STEPS

Once the perennial practices as an infrastructure are established, students use the seven-step project-based structure to conceive, manage, and deliver each individual project. Notice in Figure 11.2, each productive action a student takes in the management structure coincides with one of the seven steps.

FIGURE 11.2

Project-Based Writing 7 Steps and 16 Deliverables

Seven Steps	A Student Is...	Deliverables	What Is This?	How Is It Graded?
Discover an Idea	Discovering an idea	Writing Practice Tool	Could be a physical notebook or an online journal; student determines the source, length, and terms	Student designed rubric
Frame the Work	Pitching an idea	Pitch	Two- to five-minute oral presentation	Pitch rubric
	Proposing a product	Proposal	300–500-word informational text	Proposal rubric
Plan the Work	Stating goals for a product	Product Goals	Four sentences stating the writer's product-specific goals	Goals checklist
	Scheduling tasks for the project	Project Schedule	Calendar with projected daily goals	Schedule checklist
Do the Work	Finding supporting texts for the project	Project Library	A table where students code, summarize, and respond to various texts they select and read during the course of the project	Library checklist
	Tracking daily studio time	Project Schedule	Tracking actual daily activities on the project calendar	Schedule checklist
	Creating an inquiry draft	Inquiry draft	A completed draft of the product	Inquiry draft checklist
	Creating inquiry questions	Inquiry questions	Four questions that direct the say-back sessions	Inquiry draft checklist

continued

Seven Steps	A Student Is...	Deliverables	What Is This?	How Is It Graded?
Reframe the Work	Annotating classmates' inquiry drafts	Annotated online drafts	Evidence of annotation on all inquiry drafts	Annotation participation checklist
	Participating in say-back	Say-back participation	Participate in collaborative discussion to provide feedback to all writers	Sayback participation checklist
Finalize the Work	Creating a final product evaluative tool	Individual Evaluation Form (IEF)	Four categories by which teacher, writer, and peers evaluate the final project	Individual Evaluation checklist
	Reflecting on the project	Project reflection	300-500 argument that reflects on the product and process of the project cycle	Reflection checklist
Reveal the Work	Submitting product to community score	Final product	Product assessed by teacher	Individual Evaluation Form
			Product assessed by peers	
			Product assessed by writer	
	Participating in community score	Community score	Each student scores and submits justification for scores for all other writers in the room	Community score checklist
	Submitting the final draft to a real world audience	4P certification	Students supply proof of submission for publication, performance, production, or presentation	4P checklist

In addition to delineating student action, the framework can also easily be broken out by the "deliverables" that a student will work through for each project cycle. Deliverables are the assignments that each student completes for each step of the project cycle. Notice each student action is paired with a deliverable that can be assessed with either a checklist or a student-conceived evaluation tool.

The system of deliverables creates a measurable indicator for student growth. Students can watch their growth increase cycle by cycle as their practice improves and as they become aware of how they learn and manage projects independently. Although the quixotic notion of writers—on assignment for *Rolling Stone* or crouched over a moleskin at a Paris bistro—might be the image we get when we hear the word *writer*, the fundamentals of a writing life are decidedly unsexy. It's less about romancing the muse and more about trucking with submission guidelines as you gird your loins for endless revisions.

STANDARDS AND GRADING

The perennial questions about any kind of project-based learning concern time and grading. How do you find the time to cover all the standards? How do you grade a class of students who are all working on different projects? Let's tackle some of those questions here.

COVERING STANDARDS

In project management terms, this model constitutes a continuous improvement process that covers all Common Core standards, offering multiple opportunities for all three forms of writing, reading both literature and informational text, as well as opportunities for speaking and listening and grammar and usage instruction. Figure 11.3 is a map of the Common Core standards met by the elements of the project cycle.

Notice the overlap of standards in almost every element, because the project-based system represents the kind of open-ended, real-world learning that defines a "rich task." Skills and competencies are not taught in isolation or even in thematic units, but in a broader, cross-disciplinary approach with critical thinking and problem solving at its core (Moulds 2003).

In this way, a teacher covers skills and content multiple times throughout a project cycle, regardless of what form or purpose a student has decided to pursue. Some teachers might worry: what if Serena wants to write blog posts all year about Norwegian death metal bands? So what? All the standards in the Common Core can be met even through that ring of hell. I have students who write about fairies, hobbits, and dragons, but I also have students who write about

---

FIGURE 11.3

Common Core Standards Covered by Project-Based Writing

9.10 English Language Arts Common Core Standards										
Reading Standards for Literature										
Project-Based Objectives	Key Ideas and Details			Craft and Structure			Integration of Knowledge and Ideas			Range of Reading
	RL1	RL2	RL3	RL4	RL5	RL6	RL7	RL8	RL9	RL 10
Idea Discovery	*	*	*	*	*	*	*		*	*
Pitch										
Proposal										
Product Goals										
Project Scheduling										
Inquiry Draft										
Say-Back Session (Analysis/ Annotations)	*	*	*	*	*	*	*		*	*
Individual Evaluation Form										
Project Reflection										
Final Draft										
Community Score	*	*	*	*	*	*	*		*	*
4P										
Writing Practice										
Reading Practice (Project Library)	*	*	*	*	*	*	*		*	*

continued

history, politics, sports, agriculture, relationships, forensic pathology, fashion, and culture. All topics are on the table because the competencies laid out in the Common Core are not based in content, but in skill. Students can learn to write an argument, analyze an informational text, and parse the necromancy of the English language through any portal. Both contemporary and canonical texts are supported by this system as well, and all types of writing are represented.

9.10 English Language Arts Common Core Standards

Reading Standards for Informational Texts

Project-Based Objectives	Key Ideas and Details			Craft and Structure			Integration of Knowledge and Ideas			Range of Reading
	RI1	RI2	RI3	RI4	RI5	RI6	RI7	RI8	RI9	RI 10
Idea Discovery	*	*	*	*	*	*	*	*	*	*
Pitch										
Proposal										
Product Goals										
Project Scheduling										
Inquiry Draft										
Say-Back Session (Analysis/ Annotations)	*	*	*	*	*	*	*	*	*	*
Individual Evaluation Form										
Project Reflection										
Final Draft										
Community Score	*	*	*	*	*	*	*	*	*	*
4P										
Writing Practice										
Reading Practice (Project Library)	*	*	*	*	*	*	*	*	*	*

continued

9.10 English Language Arts Common Core Standards

Writing Standards

Project-Based Objectives	Text Types and Purposes			Production and Distribution of Writing			Research to Build and Present Knowledge			Range of Writing
	W1	W2	W3	W4	W5	W6	W7	W8	W9	W10
Idea Discovery					*	*	*	*	*	*
Pitch										
Proposal		*		*	*	*	*	*	*	
Product Goals		*		*	*	*				
Project Scheduling		*		*	*	*				
Inquiry Draft	*Project dependent*			*	*	*	*	*	*	
Say-Back Session (Analysis/ Annotations)	*			*	*	*	*	*	*	
Individual Evaluation Form		*		*	*	*	*	*	*	
Project Reflection	*					*				
Final Draft	*Project dependent*					*	*	*	*	*
Community Score	*					*				
4P	*Project dependent*									
Writing Practice				*	*	*	*	*	*	*
Reading Practice (Project Library)						*				

continued

9.10 English Language Arts Common Core Standards						
Speaking and Listening Standards						
Project-Based Objectives	Comprehension and Collaboration			Presentation of Knowledge and Ideas		
	SL1	SL2	SL3	SL4	SL5	SL6
Idea Discovery	*	*	*	*	*	*
Pitch	*	*	*	*	*	*
Proposal						
Product Goals						
Project Scheduling						
Inquiry Draft						
Say-Back Session (Analysis/ Annotations)	*	*	*	*	*	*
Individual Evaluation Form						
Project Reflection						
Final Draft						
Community Score						
4P	*Project dependent*					
Writing Practice						
Reading Practice (Project Library)						

continued

9.10 English Language Arts Common Core Standards					
Language Standards					
Project-Based Objectives	Conventions of Standard English		Knowledge of Language	Vocabulary Acquisition and Use		
	L1	L2	L3	L4	L5	L6
Idea Discovery	*	*	*	*	*	*
Pitch						*
Proposal	*	*	*	*	*	*
Product Goals	*	*	*	*	*	*
Project Scheduling	*	*	*	*	*	*
Inquiry Draft	*	*	*	*	*	*
Say-Back Session (Analysis/ Annotations)	*	*	*	*	*	*
Individual Evaluation Form	*	*	*	*	*	*
Project Reflection	*	*	*	*	*	*
Final Draft	*	*	*	*	*	*
Community Score	*	*	*	*	*	*
4P	*	*	*	*	*	*
Writing Practice						
Reading Practice (Project Library)						

DEALING WITH GRADES

I have always been disinclined to assign a numerical grade to my students' compositional efforts. What does an 82 percent mean anyway? How can you grade an expository work that clearly has matured and advanced the skill of the writer, but which still lacks proficiency in areas you value?

Alfie Kohn (1999) in *The Schools Our Children Deserve*, says, "Students who are lucky enough to be in schools (or classrooms) where they don't get letter or number grades are more likely to want to continue exploring whatever they're learning, more likely to want to challenge themselves, and more likely to think deeply" (49).

Daniel Pink agrees. In *Drive: The Surprising Truth About What Motivates Us* (2011), he says, "In fact, the evidence is overwhelming that all of the above carrots and sticks actually reduce performance and undermine motivation. When it comes to tasks that require problem solving or other right brain activities, people perform best when they are given autonomy over their tasks, opportunity for mastery in their field, and a sense that the task has a clear and meaningful purpose" (33).

In addition to Pink and Kohn's laudable reasons for not grading students' efforts, I hesitate to grade student writing, because—as one of the most complex human processes—the nuances and vicissitudes of writing are nearly impossible to anticipate or assess in the wee cells of a rubric table. In other words, the student's creativity, originality, and burgeoning processes are limited to the teacher's abilities to conceive and articulate these processes in a rubric. A traditional static rubric doesn't support the transformative nature of writing.

But rubrics do serve as a guideline of expectations. We use them because they can be good tools for feedback and measuring growth. My issue with most rubrics is that the teacher is the person who sets the expectations of a product that has yet to be created. When the teacher sets and limits the expectations for a project, the student loses twice: first, because she's been cut out of an important goal-setting process, and second, because her goals have been limited and established by someone who is not actually creating the product.

Recently a former student who had taken my project-based writing class returned to see me, bemoaning her experience of writing a personal narrative about a childhood memory in her now-traditional English class. "Our rubric says we have to state the significance of our memory in the first paragraph. We have to state the theme in the first paragraph. Then, we have to list four sensory details. There's so much planning and so much structure," she said. "I'm a writer. How am I going to pass English this year?"

And yet part of teaching is the correction of error and establishing external criteria such as formatting and deadlines that students must learn to navigate. These realities will terminate the college student who has not learned how to manage himself in high school. We aren't preparing students for the world outside our classroom if we don't teach them how to work with those carrots and sticks.

It would be great if we tossed out grades and wrote for the sake of writing. However, for a host of reasons, a nongraded class (I've tried this. Twice.) has failed to produce the kinds of skills and habits I find beneficial for growing writers. To do good work and to cultivate the management of writing projects, we all need a system of accountability that tracks our growth over time and helps us stay on task.

I use checklists and assessment tools (such as the Individual Evaluation Form) to give feedback to my students. A checklist is merely a list of characteristics that an assignment must manifest to be considered complete. A checklist does not measure quality, effectiveness, or literary or rhetorical merit; it only assures a student has met the basic external requirements of the assignment. In Figure 11.4, for example, is my proposal checklist.

A checklist is designed by the teacher and serves as a list of external requirements for a specific deliverable in the project-based writing system. An assessment tool, such as the individual evaluation form, is an instrument—designed by the student—that measures the effectiveness of a final product. Samples of the Individual Evaluation Forms can be found in Chapter 9.

FIGURE 11.4

Proposal Checklist

Proposal must include:	Points	
The genesis of the project	10	
The genre or form of the product	10	
A brief summary of the project, including purpose	10	
A measurable word count/pages/poems/chapters for manuscript goals	10	
4P goals	10	
Name, date, class/project # in upper right-/left-hand corner	10	
Typed (double-spaced, 12 pt. Times New Roman font, 1-inch margins)	10	
300–500 words	10	
Clean copy—proofread for grammar or spelling errors	10	
Submitted via Google Classroom before midnight of the due date	10	
Points Possible	**100**	

By using checklists and student-created assessment tools, a student can track his improvement at self-management while learning valuable lessons about himself as a writer without getting dinged by a teacher-created, mastery-based rubric. At the end of each project cycle, I sit down with each student and discuss his journey through the cycle using another tool I've designed to have conversations with students about their growth: the Postproject Conference Tool.

FIGURE 11.5

Postproject Conference Tool

	Not Proficient (1)	Partially Proficient (2)	Proficient (3)	Advanced (4)
Pitch	Student does not deliver the genesis, genre, summary, manuscript, and 4P goals for project within the time frame.	Student partially delivers the genesis, genre, summary, manuscript, and 4P goals for project within the time frame.	Student effectively delivers the genesis, genre, summary, manuscript, and 4P goals for project within the time frame.	Student delivers the genesis, genre, summary, manuscript, and 4P goals for the project within the time frame with clarity and complexity.
Proposal	Student does not submit the genesis, genre, summary, manuscript, and 4P goals for project in correct proposal formatting.	Student partially submits the genesis, genre, summary, manuscript, and 4P goals for project in correct proposal formatting.	Student submits the genesis, genre, summary, manuscript, and 4P goals for project in correct proposal formatting.	Student submits the genesis, genre, summary, manuscript, and 4P goals for project in correct proposal formatting with clarity and complexity.
Product Goals	Student does not establish and define four goals for the finished product.	Student partially establishes and defines four goals for the finished product.	Student establishes and defines four goals for the finished product.	Student establishes and defines four goals for the finished product with clarity and complexity.

continued

The Big Picture 193

	Not Proficient (1)	Partially Proficient (2)	Proficient (3)	Advanced (4)
Project Scheduling	Student does not create a project calendar and/or maintain a daily task tracker.	Student partially creates a project calendar and/or maintains a daily task tracker.	Student creates a project calendar and maintains a daily task tracker.	Student creates a project calendar and maintains a daily task tracker with clarity and accuracy.
Writing Practice	Student does not meet the terms of her writing contract.	Student partially meets the terms of her writing contract.	Student meets the terms of her writing contract.	Student exceeds the terms of her writing contract.
Reading Practice	Student does not meet the terms of his reading practice contract.	Student partially meets the terms of his reading practice contract.	Student meets the terms of his reading practice contract.	Student exceeds the terms of his reading practice contract.
Inquiry Draft	Student does not submit a writer's inquiry draft with correct formatting and four inquiry questions.	Student submits a partially completed writer's inquiry draft with correct formatting and four inquiry questions.	Student submits a completed writer's inquiry draft with correct formatting and four inquiry questions.	Student submits a completed and sophisticated writer's inquiry draft with correct formatting and four inquiry questions.
Say-Back Participation	Student does not participate in 50 percent of the say-back sessions.	Student participates in 70 percent of the say-back sessions.	Student participates in 90 percent of the say-back sessions.	Student participates in 100 percent of the say-back sessions and demonstrates leadership.
Reflection	Student does not submit reflection with correct formatting.	Student partially submits reflection with correct formatting.	Student submits reflection with correct formatting.	Student submits reflection with correct formatting and clarity and complexity.

continued

	Not Proficient (1)	Partially Proficient (2)	Proficient (3)	Advanced (4)
Individual Evaluation Form	Student does not create four assessment category statements.	Student partially creates four assessment category statements.	Student creates four assessment category statements.	Student creates four assessment category statements with clarity and complexity.
Final Draft: Teacher Score	*These scores are assessed and justified by the student's own Individual Evaluation Form.*			
Final Draft: Community Score				
Final Draft: Self Score				
4P	Student does not submit her writing for a 4P placement.	Student submits her writing for a 4P placement.	Student submits her writing for a 4P placement.	Student submits her writing for a 4P placement.

During the postproject conference, students gauge themselves on their ability to manage projects and their growth as a writer/reader in relation to the number of tasks in the project cycle.

Throughout the project cycle, my students and I do a lot of multifaceted formative assessments, not necessarily to gauge the student's mastery of writing but to support the student's ability to manage all of the tangible points of delivery that often will bury the writer while she's learning to write. The writing will develop naturally by the doing if one is predisposed to carry through. As I have said before, writing is its own best teacher and delivers the writer, through the act of writing itself, a sizable number of lessons if the writer is poised to listen and learn.

ON MASTERY AND FAILURE

The danger of putting out a "system" of any kind, as I witnessed firsthand with the KERA writing portfolio, is that people may come to see the system as a means to deliver gifts the system was never designed to deliver. In the 1990s, many Kentucky teachers, myself included, forgot we were teaching writers and instead taught the portfolio system. We concentrated too much on getting the system right and forgot the very thing the system is supposed to support. When one reveals a framework for teaching writing, one hopes no one will mistake the framework for the thing it supports. I want to proclaim, before we leave each other in this book, that project-based writing is not a formula for writing mastery. It is, instead, a framework for supporting failure that will assist students in self-discovery as learners, writers, and thinkers, while also giving them lifelong interpersonal skills in task and time management.

Writing is a practiced and discovered skill, its discovery born from failure, and the courage to continue grows with practice. Even among published, gifted writers, failure is the constant. Our best efforts are imperfect, and true successes in writing are those wherein we learn about our brain, our will, our psychological resilience in the face of this most complex process of creation.

Regardless of how you arrange the project management flow, the key to successfully implementing it is to give student writers multiple opportunities to practice writing to get better and better at the practice. Give students the chance to always begin again. Inasmuch as we give students chances to begin again, they are approaching mastery, even as they approach it through failure.

EVERYTHING YOU NEED

Rayny brought a two-liter bottle of Big Red to class almost every day and drank it. On the days he wasn't swigging the foamy red soda, he would drain the classroom coffee pot. A freckled, wiry farm boy with a deep gravelly voice, he was equal shares wonder and worldly. He was my village glue. If you've ever had one of these kids in your classroom, you'll recognize who I'm talking about. He was unfailingly polite and gracious to all people, including me. He signed his papers, "The Gentle Knight," but when we had some guest speakers in our classroom, he introduced himself as "The Godfather." He wrote stories about cricket fighting and voodoo. He was a philosopher-poet, a romantic in size thirteen Chuck Taylors. He had zero time management skills and would have preferred to spend all day discussing truth and beauty in my room instead of writing. At some point in the year, he decided he wanted to join the military, a decision I attempted to talk him out of. Like all of us, he contained multitudes.

During our say-back sessions, he would listen to the writer, weigh in on inquiry questions, offer general observations, occasionally push the writer to prove this or that, but always, at the end of the session, when things had wound down and it was all over but the silence and the staring, he would look around the circle until he arrived at the writer under consideration and ask, with gravity, "Do you have everything you need?"

The question was meant to ask the writer if her inquiries had been answered, if her discoveries had been fruitful, and if the community, the teacher, the system had fortified her with the substance to keep on working.

Rayny's sentence (and especially his delivery of it) became a running joke in our classroom, and because I have students who take my class year after year, some of the same students who were in that original class with Rayny have taken up the refrain, and now it's a classroom staple. The last word. The conclusion to our inquiry.

I've pondered this simple question many times and realize it is the essence of all teaching and learning. In my undergraduate years, I had the good fortune to take a class called "Composition for Teachers" taught by poet, farmer, and essayist Wendell Berry. Among other things, he read out loud to us Shakespeare's *King Lear*, the Book of Ecclesiastes, Dante's *Divine Comedy*—and he told us that bad writing would lead to boredom, tears, and shame in later life. He also told us that the job of a teacher was to arm children with tools against loneliness.

I've thought about Berry's advice in light of Rayny's question many times. Have I done enough to arm my students? Did they have everything they needed? When I think of my students—the ones I helped and the ones I didn't help—I marvel at the effort that these kids give, especially those for whom school and learning have been torture. They keep coming back even if we aren't giving them what they need to proceed as humans.

When we attempt to give kids what they need, we meet them where they are, both emotionally and at their ability levels. They need experience processing thoughts and opportunities to compose those thoughts with words, not bubbling ovals. We need to give them an infrastructure of support, so that, as my colleague Sasha Reinhardt says, freedom feels good instead of like abandonment. To give them the space to fail and the assistance to get back up. To answer their questions and ask them three in return. To give them everything they need and ask them to keep on seeking.

APPENDIX

LIST OF CRAFT BOOKS

YEARLY SERIES

Best American Series, including:

- short stories
- essays
- poetry
- sports writing
- nonrequired reading
- mystery writing
- spiritual writing
- travel writing
- nature writing
- science fiction
- fantasy.

The Art of ___ series, including:

- perspective
- recklessness
- description
- subtext
- time in fiction
- time in memoir
- intimacy

- history
- daring
- syntax.

Writing Great Fiction Series, including:

- plot and structure
- dialogue
- characters
- revision and self editing
- description and setting.

OTHER BOOKS FOR YOUR CLASSROOM LIBRARY

Addonzio, Kim, and Dorriane Laux. *The Poet's Companion*.

Atwood, Margaret. *Negotiating with the Dead: A Writer on Writing*.

Barrington, Judith. *Writing the Memoir: From Truth to Art*.

Baxter, Charles. *Burning Down the House: Essays on Fiction*.

Behn, Robin, and Chase Twichell. *The Practice of Poetry: Writing Exercises from Poets Who Teach*.

Bell, Susan. *The Artful Edit*.

Bernays, Anne, and Pamela Painter. *What If? Writing Exercises for Fiction Writers*.

Blythe, Will, ed. *On Being a Writer: Advice and Inspiration*.

Boisseau, Michelle, Robert Wallace, and Randall Mann. *Writing Poems*.

Browne, Renni, and Dave King. *Self Editing for Fiction Writers: How to Edit Yourself into Print*.

Burroway, Janet. *Imaginative Writing: The Elements of Craft*.

Burroway, Janet, and Elizabeth Stuckey-French. *Writing Fiction: A Guide to Narrative Craft*.

Cameron, Julia. *The Artist's Way: A Spiritual Path to Higher Creativity*.

Casagrande, June. *It Was the Best of Sentences, It Was the Worst of Sentences*.

Clark, Kevin. *The Mind's Eye: A Guide to Writing Poetry*.

Dillard, Annie. *The Writing Life*.

Dobyns, Stephen. *Best Words, Best Order*.

Dowst, Robert Saunders. *The Technique of Fiction Writing.*

Dufresne, John. *Is Life Like This?*

Edgar, Christopher, and Ron Padgett, eds. *Old Faithful: 18 Writers Present Their Favorite Writing Assignments.*

Egri, Lajos. *The Art of Dramatic Writing.*

Field, Syd. *The Screenwriter's Workbook.*

Forster, E. M. *Aspects of the Novel.*

Gardner, John. *The Art of Fiction.*

Goldberg, Natalie. *The True Secret of Writing.*

———. *Writing Down the Bones: Freeing the Writer Within.*

Gornick, Vivian. *The Situation and the Story.*

Grant, Reginald. *The Playwright's Guidebook: An Insightful Primer on the Art of Dramatic Writing.*

Graff, Gerald, and Cathy Birkenstein. *They Say/I Say.*

Gutkind, Lee. *The Art of Creative Nonfiction: Writing and Selling the Literature of Reality.*

Hale, Constance. *Sin and Syntax.*

Hampl, Patricia. *I Could Tell You Stories: Sojourns in the Land of Memory.*

Heard, Georgia. *Writing Toward Home: Tales and Lessons to Find Your Way.*

Hugo, Richard. *The Triggering Town.*

Iglesias, Karl. *The 101 Habits of Highly Successful Screenwriters.*

Karr, Mary. *The Art of Memoir.*

Keyes, Ralph. *The Courage to Write: How Writers Transcend Fear.*

Kidder, Tracy, and Richard Todd. *Good Prose.*

King, Stephen. *On Writing: A Memoir of the Craft.*

Kitchen, Judith, and Mary Paumier Jones, eds. *In Short: A Collection of Brief Creative Nonfiction.*

Klinkenborg, Verlyn. *Several Short Sentences About Writing.*

Kooser, Ted. *The Poetry Home Repair Manual.*

Kramer, Mark, and Wendy Call, eds. *Telling True Stories.*

Lamott, Anne. *Bird by Bird: Some Instructions on Writing and Life.*

LaPlante, Alice. *The Making of a Story.*

———. *Method and Madness.*

Le Guin, Ursula. *Steering the Craft.*

Maisel, Eric. *Fearless Creating: A Step-by-Step Guide to Starting and Completing Your Work of Art*.

McCloud, Scott. *Understanding Comics*.

McKee, Robert. *Dialogue*.

———. *Story*.

Neubauer, Bonnie. *The Write-Brain Workbook: 366 Exercises to Liberate Your Writing*.

Oates, Joyce Carol. *The Faith of a Writer: Life, Craft, Art*.

Oliver, Mary. *A Poetry Handbook*.

Percy, Benjamin. *Thrill Me*.

Pinsky, Robert. *Singing School*.

Pressfield, Steven. *The War of Art: Break Through the Blocks and Win Your Inner Creative Battles*.

Prose, Francine. *Reading like a Writer: A Guide for People Who Love Books and for Those Who Want to Write Them*.

Rabiner, Susan, and Alfred Fortunato. *Thinking Like Your Editor: How to Write Great Serious Nonfiction—and Get It Published*.

Roorbach, Bill. *Writing Life Stories: How to Make Memories into Memoirs, Ideas into Essays, and Life into Literature*.

San Francisco Writers' Grotto. *624 Things to Write About*.

———. *712 More Things to Write About*.

Schneider, Pat. *Writing Alone and with Others*.

See, Carolyn. *Making a Literary Life: Advice for Writers and Other Dreamers*.

Shapiro, Dani. *Still Writing*.

Slate, Barbara. *You Can Do a Graphic Novel*.

Smith, Michael, and Suzanne Greenberg. *Everyday Creative Writing: Panning for Gold in the Kitchen Sink*.

Stern, Jerome. *Making Shapely Fiction*.

Stoddard, David. *200 Writing Prompts*.

Strand, Mark, and Eavan Boland. *The Making of a Poem: A Norton Anthology of Poetic Forms*.

Strunk, William, and E. B. White. *Elements of Style*.

Snyder, Blake. *Save the Cat! The Last Book on Screenwriting You'll Ever Need*.

Thiel, Diane. *Winding Roads: Exercises in Writing Creative Nonfiction*.

Thomas, Frank P. *How to Write the Story of Your Life.*

Trottier, David. *Screenwriter's Bible: A Complete Guide to Writing, Formatting, and Selling Your Script.*

Tufte, Virgina. *Artful Sentences: Syntax as Style.*

Ueland, Brenda. *If You Want to Write: A Book About Art, Independence and Spirit.*

Vogler, Christopher, and Michele Montez. *The Writer's Journey: Mythic Structure for Writers.*

Welty, Eudora. *The Eye of the Story.*

Weston, Anthony. *A Rulebook for Arguments.*

Winokur, Jon, ed. *Advice to Writers: A Compendium of Quotes, Anecdotes, and Writerly Wisdom from a Dazzling Array of Literary Lights.*

Wisniewski, Mark. *Writing and Revising Your Fiction.*

Wood, James. *How Fiction Works.*

Woolf, Virgina. *Women and Writing.*

Zinsser, William. *On Writing Well.*

——. *Writing About Your Life: A Journey into the Past.*

Zinsser, William, ed. *Inventing the Truth: The Art and Craft of Memoir.*

REFERENCES

Anderson, Carl. 2000. *How's It Going?* Portsmouth, NH: Heinemann.

Applebee, Arthur N., and Judith A. Langer. 2011. "A Snapshot of Writing Instruction in Middle Schools and High Schools." *English Journal* 100 (6): 14–27.

Applebome, Peter. 2010. "Governor Christie vs. the Teachers: Nastiness in New Jersey." *The New York Times*. April 25. www.nytimes.com/2010/04/26/nyregion/26towns.html.

Atwell, Nancie. 1998. *In the Middle*. 2nd ed. Portsmouth, NH: Heinemann.

Beers, Kylene, and Robert E. Probst. 2016. *Reading Nonfiction: Notice & Note Stances, Signposts, and Strategies*. Portsmouth, NH: Heinemann.

Bell, James Scott. 2004. *Write Great Fiction: Plot and Structure*. Cincinnati, OH: Writer's Digest.

Berry, Wendell. 1982. "Poetry and Marriage." In *Standing by Words*, 204. San Francisco: North Point Press.

———. 1985. "Manifesto: The Mad Farmer Liberation Front." In *Collected Poems: 1957–1982*, 155. San Francisco: North Point Press.

———. 1993. *Sex, Economy, Freedom, & Community*. San Francisco: North Point Press.

Bly, Carol. 2001. *Beyond the Writers' Workshop*. New York: Anchor Books.

Bomer, Randy. 1995. *Time for Meaning*. Portsmouth, NH: Heinemann.

Boss, Suzie, and Jane Krauss. 2014. *Reinventing Project-Based Learning: Your Field Guide to Real-World Projects in the Digital Age*. 2nd ed. Washington, DC: Int'l Society for Technology in Education.

Calkins, Lucy McCormick. 1994. *The Art of Teaching Writing*. Portsmouth, NH: Heinemann.

Cameron, Julie. 2002. *The Artist's Way*. 10th ed. New York: Putnam.

Carey, Benedict. 2015. *How We Learn: The Surprising Truth About When, Where, and Why It Happens*. New York: Random House.

Carlson, Ron. 2007. *Ron Carlson Writes a Story*. Minneapolis, MN: Graywolf Press.

Catmull, Ed, and Amy Wallace. 2014. *Creativity, Inc.: Overcoming the Unseen Forces That Stand in the Way of True Inspiration*. New York: Random House.

Chodron, Pema. 2007. *Don't Bite the Hook*. Shambhala Publications.

Cisneros, Sandra. 1991. *The House on Mango Street*. New York: Penguin.

CNN Politics. State of the Union with Jake Tapper. 2015. "Chris Christie Interview." January 24. www.cnn.com/videos/politics/2015/08/02/sotu-tapper-christie-national-teachers-union-deserves-a-punch-in-the-face.cnn.

Coates, Ta-Nehisi. 2015. *Between the World and Me*. New York: Spiegel & Grau.

Didion, Joan. 2008 "On Keeping a Notebook." In *Slouching Towards Bethlehem*, reissue ed., 76. New York: Farrar, Straus and Giroux.

Dobson, Michael. 2010. *Creative Project Management*. New York: McGraw-Hill.

Duckworth, Angela. 2016. *Grit: The Power of Passion and Perseverance*. New York: Scribner.

Duhigg, Charles. 2014. *The Power of Habit: Why We Do What We Do in Life and Business*. New York: Random House.

Duke, Nell K., Anne-Lise Halvorsen, and Stephanie L. Strachan. 2016. "Project-Based Learning Not Just for STEM Anymore." *Phi Delta Kappan* 98 (1): 14–19.

Elbow, Peter, and Pat Belanoff. 2000. *A Community of Writers: A Workshop Course in Writing*. Boston: McGraw-Hill.

Eliot, T. S. 1986. *The Use of Poetry and Use of Criticism: Studies in the Relation of Criticism to Poetry in England (The Charles Eliot Norton Lectures)*. Cambridge, MA: Harvard University Press.

Field, Syd. 2005. *Screenplay: The Foundations of Screenwriting*. New York: Bantam Dell.

Flower, Linda, and John R. Hayes. 1981. "A Cognitive Process Theory of Writing." *College Composition and Communication* 32 (4): 365–87.

Gaiman, Neil. 2011. "Where Do You Get Your Ideas?" www.neilgaiman.com/Cool_Stuff/Essays/Essays_By_Neil/Where_do_you_get_your_ideas%3F.

Gediman, Dan. Ed. 2013. *This I Believe: Kentucky*. Butler Books.

Glenn, Cheryl. 2012. *The Harbrace Guide to Writing*. 2nd ed. Boston: Wadsworth Cengage Learning.

Godwin, Malcom. 2000. *Who Are You? 101 Ways of Seeing Yourself*. New York: Penguin.

Goldberg, Natalie. 1986. *Writing Down the Bones*. Boulder, CO: Shambhala Publications.

Gornick, Vivian. 2001. *The Situation and the Story*. New York: Farrar, Straus, and Giroux.

Toni Morrison. 2014. "Write, Erase, Do It Over" (interview by Rebecca Gross). *NEA Arts Magazine*. https://www.arts.gov/NEARTS/2014v4-art-failure-importance -risk-and-experimentation/toni-morrison.

Heard, Georgia. 2016. *Heart Maps: Helping Students Create and Craft Authentic Writing*. Portsmouth, NH: Heinemann.

Hemingway, Ernest. 1964. *A Moveable Feast*. New York: Bantam Books.

Hill, Lauryn. 1998. *The Miseducation of Lauryn Hill* (album). Ruffhouse Records.

Hillocks, George Jr. 1995. *Teaching Writing as Reflective Practice*. New York: Teachers College Press.

Hyde, Lewis. 2007. *The Gift: Creativity and the Artist in the Modern World*. New York: Vintage Books.

Kahneman, Daniel. 2011. *Thinking, Fast and Slow*. New York: Farrar, Straus and Giroux.

Kail, Thomas. 2016. Acceptance Speech—Best Direction of a Musical. https://www .youtube.com/watch?v=SEI4tWaSmKA.

Keyes, Ralph. 1995. *The Courage to Write*. New York: Henry Holt.

Kidder, Tracy, and Richard Todd. 2013. *Good Prose: The Art of Nonfiction*. New York: Random House.

King, Stephen. 2000. *On Writing: A Memoir of the Craft*. New York: Pocket Books.

Kittle, Penny. 2008. *Write Beside Them*. Portsmouth, NH: Heinemann.

Kohn, Alfie. 1999. *The Schools Our Children Deserve*. New York: Houghton-Mifflin-Harcourt.

Krajcik, Joseph S., and Phyllis C. Blumenfeld. 2006. "Project-Based Learning." In *The Cambridge Handbook of the Learning Sciences*, edited by R. Keith Sawyer. Cambridge, UK: Cambridge University Press.

Lamott, Anne. 1994. *Bird by Bird: Some Instructions on Writing and Life*. New York: Random House.

Lessons from the Screenplay. YouTube. https://www.youtube.com/channel /UCErSSa3CaP_GJxmFpdjG9Jw.

Marzano, Robert J. 2006. *Classroom Assessment & Grading That Work*. Alexandria, VA: ASCD.

Maurer, Robert. 2014. *One Small Step Can Change Your Life: The Kaizen Way*. New York: Workman Publishing Company.

McClure, Michael. 1976. Visiting Poets Academy. JKS Audio Collection. Naropa University Archives. June 16. http://cdm16621.contentdm.oclc.org/cdm/ ref /collection/p16621coll1/id/1491.

McFarlane, Evelyn, and James Saywell. 1995. *If... (Questions For The Game of Life)*. New York: Villard Books.

———. 1999. *How Far Will You Go? Questions to Test Your Limits*. New York: Villard Books.

Merwin, W. S. 2005. "Berryman." https://www.poetryfoundation.org/resources/learning/core-poems/detail/58530.

Miller, Mary Helen, et al. 1990. *A Guide to the Kentucky Education Reform Act of 1990*. Frankfort, KY: Kentucky Legislative Research Commission.

Moulds, Phillip. 2003. "Rich Tasks." *Educational Leadership* 61 (4): 75–79.

Nagao, Tadahiko, and Isamu Saito. 2000. *Kokology: The Game of Self-Discovery*. New York: Fireside.

National Governors Association Center for Best Practices and Council of Chief State School Officers. 2010. Common Core Standards. www.corestandards.org/.

Newkirk, Thomas. 2014. *Minds Made for Stories: How We Really Read and Write Informational and Persuasive Texts*. Portsmouth, NH: Heinemann.

The New York Times. "Room for Debate." https://www.nytimes.com/roomfordebate.

Pink, Daniel. 2011. *Drive: The Surprising Truth About What Motivates Us*. New York: Riverhead Books.

Popova, Maria. 2014. "William Faulkner on Writing, the Human Dilemma, and Why We Create: A Rare 1958 Recording." September 25. *Brain Pickings*. https://www.brainpickings.org/2014/09/25/william-faulkner-university-of-virginia-recording/.

Rollins, H. E., ed. 1958. *The Letters of John Keats*. Boston: Harvard University Press.

Roorbach, Bill. 2008. *Writing Life Stories*. Cincinnati, OH: Writer's Digest Books.

Rose v. Council for Better Education. 1989. National Center for Education Statistics. https://nces.ed.gov/edfin/pdf/lawsuits/Rose_v_CBE_ky.pdf.

Schneider, Pat. 2003. *Writing Alone and with Others*. New York: Oxford University Press.

ScriptLab. YouTube. https://www.youtube.com/user/thescriptlab.

Shteir, Rachel. 2014. "Failure, Writing's Constant Companion." August 15. *The New York Times*. http://opinionator.blogs.nytimes.com/2014/08/15/failure-writings-constant-companion/.

Spalding, Elizabeth, and Gail Cummins. 1998. "It Was the Best of Times. It Was a Waste of Time: University of Kentucky Students' Views of Writing Under KERA." *Assessing Writing* 5 (2): 167–99.

Stanley, Todd. 2012. *Project-Based Learning for Gifted Students: A Handbook for the 21st-Century Classroom*. Waco, TX: Prufrock Press.

Snyder, Blake. 2005. *Save the Cat: The Last Book on Screenwriting You'll Ever Need*. Studio City, CA: Michael Wiese Productions.

This I Believe. National Public Radio. 1954. "The Original Invitation from *This I Believe*." https://thisibelieve.org/history/invitation/.

Thomas, John W. 2000. *A Review of Research on Project-Based Learning*. www.ri.net/middletown/mef/linksresources/documents/researchreviewPBL_070226.pdf

Tough, Paul. 2012. *How Children Succeed: Grit, Curiosity, and the Hidden Power of Character*. New York: Houghton-Mifflin.

Trottier, David. 2014. *The Screenwriter's Bible*. 6th ed. New York: Silman-James Press.

Ueland, Brenda. 2014. *If You Want To Write*. New York: Sublime Books.

Vega, Vanessa. 2015. "Project-Based Learning Research Review." December 1. www.edutopia.org/pbl-research-learning-outcomes.

Vine Leaves Literary Journal. www.vineleavesliteraryjournal.com/.

Washington Post. 1995. "Unabomber Trial: The Manifesto." Retrieved on 12/20/2016 from www.washingtonpost.com/wp-srv/national/longterm/unabomber/manifesto.text.htm.

White, E. B. 1992. "Once More to the Lake." In *The Essays of E. B. White*, 246–55. New York: Harper-Perennial.

Whitford, Betty Lou, and Ken Jones, eds. 2000. *Accountability, Assessment, and Teacher Commitment: Lessons from Kentucky's Reform Efforts (SUNY Series, Restructuring and School Change)*. Albany, NY: State University of New York Press.